TELL IT TO THE MARINES

TELL IT TO THE MARINES

A Royal Marines Ragbag

Edited by
Michael McConville

Sponsored by the 1664 Club

CHIVERS LARGE PRINT
BATH

British Library Cataloguing in Publication Data available

This Large Print edition published by Chivers Press, Bath, 1997.

Published by arrangement with the Friends of the Royal Marines
Museum.

U.K. Hardcover ISBN 0 7540 3072 5

The 1664 Club and the editor gratefully acknowledge the helpfulness in
granting permission to publish copyright material of: George Weidenfeld
& Nicholson Limited for the extract, printed here as 'A Domestic Day
With The Brigadier', from *The Diaries of Evelyn Waugh*, Ed. Michael
Davie. André Deutsch, Ltd., for the extract from *One Marine's Story* by
General Sir Leslie Hollis, printed here as *A Day On The Ocean Wave*.
Bryan Samain and his publishers Lionel Leventhal Ltd. for the extract,
printed here as 'Crossing the Rhine', 23 March, 1945, from Bryan
Samain's *Commando Men*. John Day, from whose *A Plain Russet-Coated
Captain*, the piece printed as 'Amateur Status' has been filched and
greatly compressed. Daphne Freeman, *The Adjutant Bird* from a Punch
article of hers. They would also like to thank Giles, JAK and Smiles for
permission to reproduce their cartoons.

Photoset, printed and bound in Great Britain by
Redwood Books, Trowbridge, Wiltshire

FOREWORD
by
Sir John Harvey-Jones, MBE

'Tell It To The Marines' is a well known saying, especially in the Naval service in which I served for 20 years, alongside Royal Marines on many occasions. The understanding of the origins of the phrase by many of my naval colleagues was to the effect that the Royals, as we affectionately knew them, would believe anything. Their belief of its origin goes back to King James II, who is alleged to have said to an aide that a certain theory be tested by asking his recently formed Corps of sea soldiers; if they believed it, then it must be right, he said.

Whatever the truth, there is no doubt in my mind that they are not only the finest Corps in the world but they have a long history of achievement for King, Queen and Country since 1664 when they were formed. I never hear a Royal Marines Band, or watch the Marines at Ceremonial, without a frisson of pride and affection. As many a soldier or sailor can tell you, during the heat of battle or whilst preparing for it, probably in lengthy periods of training and often far from home, there are many funny moments which are most often the memories we prefer to recall.

In this book of Marines' tales are many such

stories that may well be apocryphal and almost certainly embroidered in the telling over the decades. In it you will find much to laugh over and see just one side of this great Corps, their sense of humour which may well be against themselves but which has kept them going in conditions which most of us would find appalling.

Sponsored by the 1664 Club, the Friends of the Royal Marines' very fine museum in Portsmouth, the profits will go to adding to its record of the Corps's history of the most recent events including the epic battle for the recovery of the Falklands in which the Corps played a leading part as custodians of Britain's amphibious capability.

I commend this book to anyone wanting a good laugh to cheer themselves up in what is so often seen to be a terrible world.

John Harvey-Jones

CONTENTS

PART I
First Person Singular

vii

PART II
Third Person, Singular and Plural

RIGHT! Knock it off. Just because the Royal Marines are playing at Wembley instead of the Guards.

EDITOR'S NOTE

As Sir John Harvey-Jones points out in his Foreword, the term 'Tell It To The Marines' has down the centuries become distorted in meaning. It does not, as popular usage has it, refer to the naive credulity of simple-minded marines. Rather, it meant originally that if you were doubtful about the authenticity of some plausible but improbable story you took it for assessment to a marine, whose wisdom and experience would ensure a reliable judgement.

Whether or not all the stories in this compilation are of similar reliability is a matter for the reader to decide for himself. The book is not about anyone telling anything to the marines. It is the marines, and associated friends, who do the telling. Since, in most cases, there are few people still around who are qualified to comment upon the accuracy of the events recorded it might just be that here and there an element of poetic licence has crept in. Only an unreconstructed oaf would be crass enough to try to identify these deficiencies; if indeed they exist, which is not admitted.

The book's sponsors are the 1664 Club, the Friends of the Royal General Marine's Museum. When the Club's Chairman, Major General Bob Loudoun, put out an appeal to serving and past members of the Corps for reminiscent stories the response was so large that, regrettably, more have had to be omitted from the collection than are included in it. The 1664 Club, and I personally who enjoyed them all and had the hard task of deciding what should go in and what stay out, are grateful to every contributor. Published or not, all stories have been preserved by the Club for presentation to the Museum's archives.

A last word of thanks to Major Peter Thompson, RM, of the 1664 Club Council, who with patient and good-humoured efficiency steered the book through its production and printing processes; and to Captain Victor Pegler, RM, the Hon. Secretary of the Club, and his assistant Mrs Jill Wynn-Potts, who handled a great deal of administrative work with cheerful despatch.

Michael McConville, August 1993

PART ONE

FIRST PERSON SINGULAR

BLOOD BROTHER

*The Rt. Hon. Paddy Ashdown MP: Captain,
Royal Marines; Parliamentary Leader,
Liberal Democrats*

When I was in the SBS, we used to dive off the east coast of Malaya at a very beautiful island called Pulau Tioman.

The water here was exceptionally clear and the sea bed very beautiful. The disadvantage was that it was a breeding ground for sharks. One never dived without seeing a shark of some sort or another. Nothing very big. Six foot appeared to be about the limit. Furthermore, whilst every ship that had ever come to Pulau Tioman always used the bathing facilities, nobody in the whole history of the place had ever been taken by a shark.

The danger was, therefore, minimal.

However, there is something absolutely terrifying about rounding rocks under water and seeing a shark. You in your clumsy diving suit and breathing apparatus and this thing eyeing you with such sleek power and speed, you feel totally out of place. In short, the sight of a shark, however large, always set the heart beating a little faster.

One day, when preparing to go for a dive with my "buddy", Marine Peter X, I noticed

3

that he was wearing a sharp stick. I asked him what it was. He said, 'This is my shark stick, Sir'. I told him not to be ridiculous and that the stick would not keep off a shark. His reply was, 'It's not designed to, Sir. It's to poke you and make you bleed so that I have time to get away'!

THE FASTEST LONG-HAIRED DJ IN THE WEST

Sir James Savile, OBE Television Presenter; Charity Fund Raiser

One of the most unlikely double acts in the world has to be the Royal Marines and a long-haired disc-jockey.

It all started innocently enough with my eldest brother, Vince, a CPO Cox'n in the Royal Navy. We had just done the 50 mile London to Brighton walk. Top of the Pops filmed the effort and fifteen million people saw it. Including the public relations boys at Lympstone.

A phone call from brother Vince, 'The Royal Marines want to know if we want to do their thirty-miler across Dartmoor.' 'Wow' says I, 'that's an honour plus it's twenty miles less than the London—Brighton.' 'Be careful' warned big brother—'they're quite ruthless

4

and you could finish up quite dead.'

And It Came To Pass, as it says in the good Book, that about six a.m. of a clear August morning in the hamlet of Belstone in Dartmoor that the world's most unlikely double act took place.

The dreaded thirty-miler of the equally dreaded Royal Marines.

The story of that day is a spectacular saga of survival to be told another time but suffice to say that just under eight hours later, with two recruits on their way to hospital because of the intense August heat, a long-haired figure, surrounded by short-haired figures, appeared high on the hillside overlooking Buckfastleigh.

The PR lads had done their stuff and every British newspaper was there plus the television.

It was exactly at that time the problem arose and exactly the reason that, thirty years later, I am still an adopted regular at Lympstone.

It started with an innocent remark from a journalist. 'If the Royal Marines are so tough, how come a disc jockey can make their top challenge?' Terrible dawning realisation from the top brass. How to answer such a simple question. To shoot me and hide the body would be good but there were too many witnesses. The day was saved in real Royal Marine style by Captain Chris Goode who strolled across to me as I lay in the hedge and hissed, 'You're not a civilian any more, you're an honorary Royal Marine recruit.' This

5

information he duly gave out to the assembled press.

'Worry not' said the resourceful Chris, 'we can get him to do the rest of the Green Beret course and kill him when no-one is looking.'

But, craftiness is not reserved entirely for the Corps.

Over the following year and a half as and when the Corps PR wanted and my diary permitted, we picked off all the items needed. By now the media had got the bug and followed everything we did. The endurance course made national television as did the Tarzan course. Big problem, when was I going to die. With the nine-miler left to do there was a sudden halt to the proceedings. For over a year I heard nothing from the camp. So I turn my Mensa logic on and phone brother Vince. 'How's everybody at Lympstone?' 'O.K.' says Vince. 'They ring me once a month.' 'Next time they phone and ask about me' says I, 'tell them I've started drinking, smoking too much and got a belly.'

The trap sprung. I got a call from the camp. 'Hi Jim, can you do the nine-miler in the next couple of weeks?' It was a shame to take the money. Seventy eight minutes instead of the required ninety is nearly a course record.

I had my own passing out parade in Exmouth. Ten thousand people turned up for the fund raising day and I became the one and only civilian—still—to get the coveted Green

Beret.

PS. If any other civvy gets anywhere near, I will personally shoot him and hide the body.

DEPTH OF EMOTION

Sir John Harvey-Jones, MBE: Royal Navy; Industrialist; Television Business Analyst

I was serving as a first lieutenant on the frigate *St Austell Bay* and we were making passage across the Atlantic from Plymouth to Bermuda. Somewhere roundabout the middle of the Atlantic where the depth of the water is a little over 3,000 feet, we stopped the ship and piped hands to bathe. Although only a frigate, we were at that time carrying the first Royal Marine detachment to garrison the Falkland Islands. My sailors all leapt over the side with happy cries shortly to be followed by the Royal Marines in a slightly more disciplined manner. I was on the quarter deck at the time and saw to my dismay that one of the Marines having jumped in, immediately sank. He came up again spluttering and yelling for help, only moments later to disappear smartly beneath the water again. With a fair amount of difficulty we eventually hauled him out and pumped the water out of him on the quarter deck. I remember being a little peeved at the

7

time and saying to him—you silly B, why the hell did you jump in if you couldn't swim? He looked at me in a perplexed manner and said 'I didn't think it would be so deep Sir'.

GOOD NEWS IS WHAT YOU THINK HE SAID

Angela Rippon: Television Presenter;
Daughter of Long-Service Royal Marine

A few years ago, the R.S.P.C.A. wanted to make a presentation to the Royal Marines stationed at the Stonehouse Barracks in Plymouth, in recognition of their work in helping to rescue animals on Dartmoor after an especially bleak winter.

They asked me to make the presentation on their behalf in Stonehouse, and the Commanding Officer suggested that it might be a good idea for me to be collected from my home on Dartmoor by helicopter, and flown into the barracks. The local boys' public school, Kelly College, allowed us to use their playing fields as a landing pad, so I had only a few minutes drive from my home, and then the crew took me on a trip around the moor to see some of the terrain from a 'birds eye' view.

It was incredibly noisy, in spite of the ear muffs, so that by the time we approached

Plymouth Sound, and dropped down onto the parade square inside Stonehouse, I was almost completely deaf. As I got out of the helicopter the C.O. made a short speech of welcome, to which I had to reply. Unfortunately because of the temporary deafness I couldn't hear a word … just watched his lips moving! I can only hope that my reply made sense, because to this day I haven't a clue about what he actually said!

A DOMESTIC DAY WITH THE BRIGADIER

Evelyn Waugh: Writer, Commissioned, at the age of thirty-six, as a Royal Marine Second Lieutenant in December, 1939

In February, 1940, whilst training at Kingsdown in Kent, Waugh first set eyes upon his future Brigade Commander, Brigadier St Clair Morford, '… who looks like something escaped from Sing Sing and talks like a boy in the fourth form at school—teeth like a stoat, ears like a faun, eyes alight like a child playing pirates: "We have to biff them, gentlemen." He scares half and fascinates half.'

By the end of the month Waugh was at Bisley. From his diary for 26 February, 1940:

9

I decided to remain in camp this weekend as a measure of economy. On Thursday the Brigadier appeared in our tent where we were stripping the Bren and told Messer-Bennetts that we were to spend the day with him on Saturday. He picked us up at 12.30 and, driving all over the road, took us to a depraved villa of stockbroker's Tudor. I asked if he had built it himself. 'Built it? It's four or five hundred years old.' That was a bad start. He turns slate-grey instead of red when he is angry. Inside the villa there was evidence that the nucleus of the house had been an old cottage. Mrs Morford was pretty and bright. She seems to me to lead a peculiar life with the Brigadier. She told us with great relish how, the night before, she had to get up several times to look after a sick child. Each time the Brigadier laid a booby trap against her return by putting his boots on the top of the door. He shouts, 'Woman, get the cigarettes!' and she trots off cheerfully. Most of the Brigadier's family reminiscences dealt with floggings he administered or with grave accidents resulting from various dangerous forms of holiday-making. After luncheon, we went for a walk in fine weather and fine country round Sutton Place. He said that he missed his hockey in wartime. Golf was not the same thing; nor rackets (at which his wife excelled) 'One has to play team games as long as one possibly can. Last war I was centre-half for my company. It was worth £100 a minute. You get hold of your men that way. I had hold of my men. If a man was brought up before me for a crime, I used to say, "Will you have a court-martial or take it from me?" They always took it from me. I bent 'em over and gave 'em ten as tight as I could. My company had the best record for crime in the regiment.

We went back to tea and a new daughter arrived from London, very large and attractive. The Brigadier turned grey several times with this daughter, who was by a previous madam and a Catholic. She has a job in London but, said the Brigadier, was infected by the younger generation's craving for change and pleasure. She told me that she had been a liftgirl in the Times Book Club and lost her job because, at Christmastime, she hung mistletoe in the lift. The Brigadier thought it most unsuitable that she should tell me that. After tea the Brigadier produced a book of verses and drawings compiled by himself and his wife in imitation of the *Just So Stories* and the *Book of Beasts*. I had to read all these verses with the B. breathing stertorously down my neck. Many of them dealt with waking people in the morning with cold sponges. 'That really happened to my wife's brother Ivor,' he said. A number of majors came in to dinner, all with their madams, all foreign, a coincidence on

11

Unrecorded History

Telling it to the Marines aboard *HMS Taradiddle* of the decision of HM
Government to evacuate Egypt at an early date—say 1st April 1897

which the Brigadier did not fail to comment rather frequently. "Extraordinary thing these Marine officers' wives—one Russian, one Swede, one a Hun. I pulled Mrs Mac's leg about Sweden the other day. Said they were all skunks. She was quite annoyed." We had plenty to eat and drink.

Candle-shades and table-mats painted by Mrs Morford, some with Japanese flowers, others with lanterns.

After dinner the Brig. and I talked of Africa. He told me of a Gyppy he could trust, the only one in the country, Hassamir (?) Bey, an adviser of Farouk's. This unhappy man had once had to spend a day travelling with the Brig. in a train from Luxor, single track, narrow gauge, desert on both sides and intense heat. The Brig. thought he would go mad. Luckily he had a golf ball with him so he and the Gyppy played ball all the way 'throwing it as hard as he could, so that it jolly well hurt'. The Gyppy kept it up all day. Not many could have done that, 'I never saw him again but it made a great impression on me. He was a white man.'

He drove us back all the way, picking up a number of Canadians, Guardsmen and assorted stragglers on the way, and then returned to start his office work at home.

WHERE DID YOU GET THAT HAT?

General PX Kelly: Commandant, United States Marine Corps; served on an exchange secondment to The Royal Marines

During Operation Pony Express, a joint US/UK exercise in Borneo during the Spring of 1961, I was serving as the Commanding Officer, 'C' Troop, 42 Commando. The day before the actual helicopter landing, the Commanding General of the U.S. Marine Corps Brigade visited 42 Commando aboard HMS Bulwark for an orientation tour. Upon his arrival, the Commanding Officer of 42 presented him with a Green Beret as a gesture of friendship. Passing down the line of officers on the flight deck, he noted the U.S. Marine Corps emblem on my beret and said: 'I see we have another U.S. Marine wearing a Green Beret.' Saluting smartly I responded: 'Yes, Sir, but I earned mine.' Not another word was spoken.

DEPOT AT LYMPSTONE

Ron Todd: Late General Secretary, Transport and General Workers Union. Royal Marines, 1945–1947

During Recruit Training in 1945 at the Depot at Lympstone:

*   *   *

We had all been assembled in the camp cinema to be addressed on the subject of personal body fitness by two veteran sportsmen. One was the ex Fly Weight champion, Jimmy Wilde, and the other sportsman was the ex one mile record holder, Joe Binks, who then wrote for the News of the World. During the lectures many of us found it difficult, in the warm atmosphere of the cinema, to keep our eyes open and focused on the speakers. Eventually some of us succumbed to the temptation and dozed off.

At the end of the lectures, following the appropriate vote of thanks to the speakers and their departure, Quartermaster Sergeant Instructor Chivers addressed us from the stage. He said that during the lectures he had noticed that a number of recruits had lacked concentration and appeared tired and listless. He went on to say that he believed he could assist us with this problem. He had a remedy. He then instructed the non-commissioned officers to disperse all ranks to their huts where we were to don full kit with rifles and return to the parade ground.

When we re-assembled on the parade area, suitably kitted, we found that the Royal Marine Band were also in attendance. QMSI Chivers stood out in front rubbing his palms together and with his ninety decibels throat, roared 'What's a nice lively tune?' and without pausing for any response (who would dare) he instructed the Band Master to play Pop Goes the Weasel. As the band struck up, the command was given to double march, and around and around the square with rifles on our shoulders we went for what seemed an eternity, but in truth, how many times we did circle or for how long, I cannot recall. I only remember pounding around while in your mind you had the regular beat of:

Half a pound of tuppenny rice
Half a pound of treacle
That's the way the money goes
Pop goes the weasel

When we were finally halted and 'dressed our ranks', QMSI Chivers stood in front of the squad and asked if anyone felt tired or listless.

We were then dismissed and we crawled back to our huts, collapsed onto our bunks

16

(still fully kitted) and contemplated with some enthusiasm the kind of fate that we would wish to overtake QMSI Chivers, at the same time laughing at each others' discomfort.

THE ADJUTANT BIRD

Daphne Freeman: Wartime Wren, Married to Captain Tony Crockett, the Adjutant at Eastney Barracks, Portsmouth

They left the Adjutant's residence for work each morning within a few minutes of each other; he to the parade ground 'resplendent in glassy creaking leather, shimmering brasses, faultless uniform'; she 'a huddled collection of blue serge—the general issue of bell-bottoms for small male sailor, the soft shapeless Wren beret ... and an unpressed greatcoat that smelled of the dust of railway trains and canteens', heading on a dilapidated bicycle to unglamorous toil at Frazer Battery. The difference of status during working hours generated some complexities:

There were two other occasions when he might well have had cause to regret marrying so far beneath him. One was the usual inspection of heads for livestock from which nobody was exempt. I found I had to go with the rest when I was supposed to accompany my

17

husband to the Junior N.C.O.s' Boxing Finals—an Important Affair.

Seeing Tony sitting alone in a ring-side seat the General, I gather, called across in the booming voice that all good generals affect—'Your good lady not here, my boy?'

Presumably dazzled by the thought of possessing a Good Lady, Tony responded brightly—'No, sir, she's having her head looked into at Fort Cumberland.'

The other occasion was when the Adjutant put his foot down about the disgraceful slackness amongst the rankers in not carrying their pay books with them. He threw in his small army of Military Police, and with two trucks they waited on strategic corners and vital gates to catch the unwary.

They apparently had a dull time of it until they netted me, ambling home in the evening sunlight pay-bookless and unrepentant.

'You'll have to go along to the Adjutant's office,' they told me grimly, as if he were sitting there in wait with thumb-screws and rack for offenders, whereas I knew he was having his hair cut by a corporal in the spare room of what was officially known as the Adjutant's residence.

Seeing that I was undismayed; in fact overjoyed, they asked my official number, my establishment and finally what right had I to be in the barracks at all.

'Oh, I'm going to the Adjutant's house,' I

18

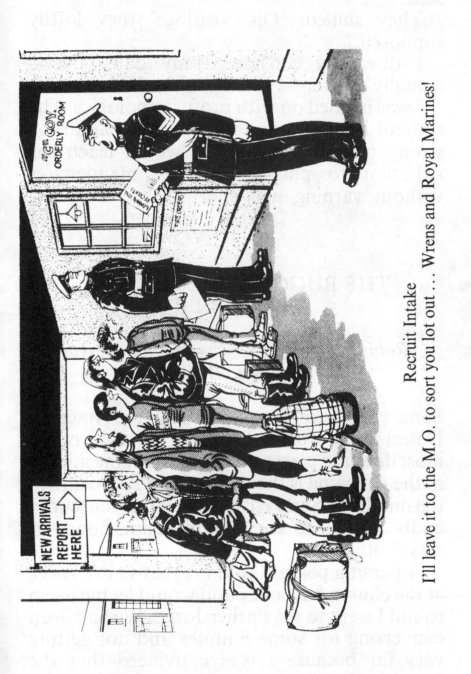

Recruit Intake

I'll leave it to the M.O. to sort you lot out . . . Wrens and Royal Marines!

19

said.

They smiled. 'Oh, visiting?' they loftily supposed.

I discreetly considered my nails. 'No—actually—I—er—I live with him.'

I was hustled on with profuse apologies. The code of honour amongst men is apparently a strong one. I thought that would teach the Adjutant to put on military manoeuvres without warning me.

THE BUGGERS HAUNT YOU WHEREVER

Robin Neillands: 45 Commando, Royal Marines. Writer

Some years ago I found myself in the Atacama Desert in the North of Chile. This is one of the most desolate places on earth but in the middle of the Atacama is the oasis of San Pedro and in the middle of San Pedro was a small museum I badly wanted to see. The museum, however, was shut.

A passing peasant told me that Padre Jorge at the church had a key and would let me in, so round I went to see Father Jorge. We had been conversing for some minutes and not getting very far because I was convinced that the Spanish word for key was 'abula' which

20

actually means 'grandmother'. Since Father Jorge did not have any grandmothers to hand we were a bit at a loss. Eventually he asked 'Are you English?' and I said 'Yes, are you?' and he said 'No, I'm from Malta'.

End of problem, I thought, 'I know Malta well'. I said happily, 'My unit was stationed there for years.'

A wary look crept into Father Jorge's eyes 'What unit was that?'

'45 Commando ... Royal Marines.'

Father Jorge aged suddenly. 'I came all the way from Malta to this howling wilderness' he said, 'and three weeks after I get here there is a Royal Marine on my doorstep, looking for his grandmother ...'

A DAY ON THE OCEAN WAVE

General Sir Leslie Hollis, KCB, KBE.
Commandant General, Royal Marines,
1949–51

In 1926 I was appointed to the battleship *Revenge*, the flagship of the Atlantic Fleet, of which Admiral Sir Henry Oliver was Commander-in-Chief. Soon after joining her I had a very eventful day. The occasion was our arrival at Vigo during that year's spring cruise after a rough crossing of the Bay of Biscay.

21

Commander W. S. Chalmers, D.S.O., R.N., who had joined the ship with me at Portsmouth a week or two earlier, told me that he expected the Royal Marine guard and band to show its paces when the Admiral went ashore the following morning to return the courtesy call which the Spanish Governor of Vigo had paid on our arrival. Next day there was much activity on board, with decks being scrubbed and brass-work polished. The awning was spread and in due course the Commander-in-Chief's guard and band were paraded. Both were Royal Marines. The time-honoured ceremonial which accompanies a Commander-in-Chief's departure from his flagship on an official call was observed. Quartermasters, bosun's mates with their pipes. Royal Marine corporals of the gangway, and side-boys took up their appointed stations. Aft of them and under the awning were the Royal Marine guard and band with the 15-inch guns of the Royal Marine turret looming out above.

When all was ready, the Flag Lieutenant-Commander, Douglas Lang, reported to the Commander-in-Chief, who duly arrived on deck to the accompaniment of a fanfare by the band and a salute by the guard. After complimenting me on the turn-out of the guard, the admiral, a bearded figure, went to the gangway and stepped over the side while the bosuns piped and everyone stood to attention.

As Admiral Oliver went down the ladder, a huge tin of metal polish flashed past his nose from the awning, cascading liquid in the stern-sheets of his immaculate barge. Strong men swayed and weaker men wilted, but silence continued to reign. The admiral picked his way through a sea of polish and stood at the salute while his barge drew away from the ship.

As soon as the bugler sounded Carry on, a storm was let loose on the quarterdeck. It was clear that somebody belonging to Royal Marines' turret was responsible for the outrage. After falling out the officers and dismissing the guard and band, I went to the port side of the quarter-deck, where a corporal, with two Marines in overalls accompanied by my Detachment sergeant-major, were already waiting. Their mien was dejected. I asked the corporal to report. He said that, as I was aware, the passage of the Bay had been rough and an extra layer of grease had consequently been applied to the two shining muzzles of the 15-inch guns in the Royal Marine turret. It had therefore taken the two Marines concerned longer than usual to remove the grease. One of them, Parkes, lying stretched out on the muzzle of the gun, felt himself losing his balance on the greasy surface. It was, he claimed, a question of whether he should go over the side or the tin of polish. Using his own initiative, the corporal continued, Parkes in difficult circumstances had shown the correct judgment usually credited to the Royal Marines. Rather than that he should flash past the astonished Commander-in-Chief's nose, was it not better that the tin of polish should go? Parkes decided on the latter course; and in the corporal's opinion, Parkes had done the right thing; indeed, he was to be commended.

I could not but be impressed by this argument. I did not feel that anything Parkes had done deserved credit; but I did incline to the view that no disciplinary action was called for, I therefore said that for the remainder of the commission Parkes was to be relegated to the shell-room, and that he was never again to be allowed on the quarter-deck, let alone on the awning, when any ceremonial was going on. When the hearing was finished the sergeant-major dismissed the three Marines.

But the affair was not finished. When I reappeared on the starboard side of the *Revenge* the Flag Captain, Colvin, demanded that the miscreants should be immediately arraigned before him. I said that I had already examined those responsible and had dismissed them with a strongly-worded caution. Colvin took a dim view of what I had done.

My assertion that the case had been dismissed and therefore could not be re-opened, did nothing to improve matters. The Commander, Chalmers, who was also present and had a great sense of humour, was at some pains to conceal his amusement, while at the

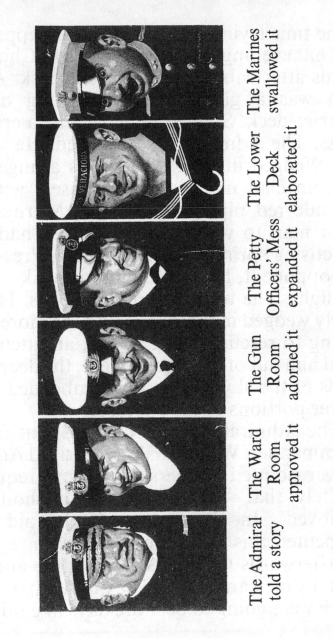

| The Admiral | The Ward Room | The Gun Room | The Petty Officers' Mess | The Lower Deck | The Marines |
| told a story | approved it | adorned it | expanded it | elaborated it | swallowed it |

same time trying to show strong disapproval.

That evening the Commander-in-Chief was in his after-cabin working at his desk. Above him was a glass skylight opening on the quarter-deck. Suddenly there came a crash of glass. The Admiral was showered. He looked up. Wedged in the skylight was a huge male bottom clad in navy blue trousers with the tell-tale red piping of a Royal Marine. The poor man to whom they belonged had been practising spring-bayonet fighting. Pressed by his opponent, he had caught his hocks on the skylight. The results were disastrous. He was fairly wedged in the glass—and the more those trying to rescue him heaved in an attempt to haul him out of his predicament, the deeper the glass of the skylight became embedded in the softer portions of his anatomy.

The Admiral rang his bell and sent for the Commander. When Chalmers arrived Admiral Oliver pointed to the skylight and requested politely that 'this fighting man should be removed'. In the end, with the aid of a carpenter, this was done.

Afterwards Chalmers sent for me and said that my men and I would be the death of him if there were going to be more days like this one.

FORCES PROGRAMME: DIFFERENT WAVELENGTH

Nick Demuth: Musician; Machine Gun Officer of No. 43 Royal Marine Commando when they returned briefly to Italy from Yugoslavia in the autumn of 1944

When we arrived in Putignano from Vis, I decided the members of F Troop needed a Radio. A quick recce round the town showed that there was nothing—literally—in any of the shops so I decided the only thing to do was to rent one.

Equipping myself with an instant English-Italian phrase book I set off.

'Excuse me' I said 'I would like to hire a Radio.'

Although I thought I was speaking Italian, the Putignanoese reacted in a positively negative way.

They bowed, they smiled, they hurried past and veered away but answer received I none until a small cheerful urchin of a kind that Italy was bursting at the seams with during the war years, greeted me with a grin and a bright 'Hello Joe'.

He seemed to have no trouble with my London-accented Italian and saying 'OK Joe' set off at a lively pace down a nearby side street. We eventually stopped at a house which had seen better days and mounted to the second floor.

Without bothering to knock, he flung the door open revealing a spotlessly clean if a trifle shabby room mostly filled with a dining room table, an elderly couple and a young girl. They looked at me blankly as I equally blankly looked round for a radio. I smiled and repeated my well-worn and only sentence in Italian.

With a bow and a flourish of one hand my guide proudly announced: 'Signorina, she f . . . s!'

The lads in F Troop never did get a Radio!

ROYAL FLUSH

Lieutenant Colonel Sir Vivian Dunn, KCVO, OBE, RM: Director of Music, Royal Marines; Pastmaster The Worshipful Company of Musicians

In 1934 the Admiralty quite rightly introduced the English Hymnal to replace Hymns Ancient and Modern for service in the Royal Navy. Sunday church in the Royal Yacht Victoria and Albert was always important for the band, to ensure the smooth running of the service. King George V and Queen Mary always attended and I used to cast a wary eye to see

28

that all was well.

The King carried a beautiful gold-bound ivory prayer book and when the first hymn was announced as 165, he opened at the number required but seemed puzzled as if he had not heard the number correctly. Turning the pages to 265 and finding this no better he remained solemnly silent. This happened again with the other two hymns and he looked very cross. After the service he sent for the Admiral and complained: 'What was the matter with the hymns this morning? I couldn't find my place.' The Admiral did not know and turned to me for the answer which I suspected. I checked to find the hymn numbers were different in both books.

On being given this information he furiously commented: 'There's a fine thing. Here am I, Defender of the Faith, and I wasn't even consulted!'

CROSSING THE RHINE.
23 MARCH, 1945

Bryan Samain. Writer and Public Relations Consultant. Intelligence Officer, 45 Commando, North West Europe, 1944–45. No. 1 Commando Brigade (3 and 6 Army Commandos, 45 and 46 Royal Marine Commandos) crossed the Rhine at Wesel in the Spring of 1945

At seven o'clock that night, three hours before H Hour, the whole of our Brigade was formed up on the western bank of the Rhine. Everyone lay about in scattered groups, their faces blackened, green berets on their heads—we never wore tin helmets—and laden with assault equipment.

During those last hours before we went over rum and biscuits were served out, together with the mail, which we all tried very hard to read in the darkness, by the light of carefully concealed candles and hurricane lamps. Meanwhile, the Buffaloes [*Tracked Armoured Personnel Carriers*] began to arrive on the road leading towards the river.

At eight o'clock the Gunners opened up their 'softening programme' on Grav Insel. Within the space of seconds the air was filled with the angry rumble of heavy guns, the

30

thunderous roar of nearby 25-pounder Regiments, the pop-popping of hundreds of mortars, and the insistent chatter of Vickers machine-guns.

A few hundred yards in front of us the slim ribbon that was the Rhine became almost hidden with the reddish bursts of thousands of shells, each of which left thick, weaving clouds of smoke. Away to the right, around Wesel, it seemed as if thousands of candles had been lighted and suspended like so many fairy lights over the town as orange-coloured tracer shells from light anti-aircraft guns curved in a series of graceful parabola towards their targets. The dull night sky gleamed strangely with a ruddy glow as fires were started.

Whilst all this was going on, a B.B.C. commentator—who shall be nameless—was

Recovering L.C.A.'s

wandering around the Buffaloes, talking to our men and asking them various questions, microphone in hand. From one young North Country Marine to whom he put the rather ridiculous question, 'Do you think you'll be first across?' the answer came pat enough: 'Not if I can bloody well help it, mate.'

After that, the B.B.C. man completely disappeared.

THIRD PERSON,
SINGULAR AND PLURAL

PART TWO

THIRD PERSON:
SINGULAR AND PLURAL

NOT DEAD, BUT GONE BEFORE

There were instances, it seemed to the young Second Lieutenant Hollis, in which the policy of looking after ageing officers who had once been good, but were by now burnt out, was pressed beyond the bounds of acceptable generosity.

A case in point arose at Stonehouse Barracks in Plymouth in 1914. Hollis was detailed off as the junior officer with a funeral party. The party, wearing Number 1 Dress, was fallen in on the Parade. The coffin was on a handcart. In command of the party was a plump elderly captain, sweating heavily on a hot day. He gave his orders adequately. The cortege set out to march to Crownhill Cemetery, the handcart in front pushed by two marines, the escort stepping out smartly behind.

After a few hundred yards the fat captain ordered a halt. He produced a hip flask, and refreshed himself generously. The march was resumed. It was interrupted by further halts of increasing frequency until the hip flask was finally emptied.

There was another, prolonged, delay at the cemetery itself. The captain fell into the grave ahead of the coffin. The supervision of his extrication and of his replacement by the coffin, the first conducted in a disciplined manner and the second with reverence, together gave Second Lieutenant Hollis a testing challenge to his powers of leadership.

THOUGHT OF THIS ONE MARIE STOPES?

A four battalion-strong Royal Marine Brigade—the battalions designated Chatham, Plymouth, Portsmouth and Deal—fought ashore in the Royal Naval Division throughout the First World War. In May, 1915, the Division issued a general order to be promulgated to all ranks.

The heading read: BABIES: PRECAUTIONS AGAINST. The first in a numbered list of contraceptive measures to be taken was the immediate shooting of all stray dogs.

Before too many marines had the chance to put this new form of birth control to the test a short amendment to the order followed, also to be promulgated to all ranks.

'FOR BABIES,' it stated, 'READ RABIES.'

THE TEETH OF THE MATTER

Surgeon Lieutenant Sparrow was the doctor of the Plymouth Battalion of the Royal Marine Light Infantry in 1916 during the protracted and bloody Somme fighting. He crawled out one morning through the mud to succour a badly wounded marine who was lying in the open in the midst of a heavy artillery barrage.

Sparrow reached his patient. He was suffering from multiple wounds, the most noticeable of which was a fractured jaw. Sparrow carried out a brief medical

Royal Naval Division

France 1916

Up Anchor!

examination. He concluded that unless the victim could be got back quickly he would face three possible fates: he would die from his wounds; he would be killed by a shell; or he would die from exposure.

The patient seemed to be unconcerned by any of these prospects. He had another major worry on his mind.

'Is my false teeth alright?' he asked anxiously. 'They cost me two pounds three and nine before the war.'

TURKISH HOT POT

Major Norman Burge, commanding the Cyclists Company of the Royal Naval Division in May 1915 at Gallipoli, moved his command, long since separated from its bicycles, to a small vineyard sited in what passed in the peninsula for a reserve position.

Burge was confronted suddenly by a suspicious-looking, scruffy character clasping a rifle and lurking in the shadow of a bush. Turkish snipers had persistently infiltrated into the area. Burge drew his pistol, and asked the man menacingly who he was. The man replied in a strange, unintelligible tongue. His suspicions confirmed, Burge grabbed the man's rifle and roared for his orderly.

The lurker let out a terrified yell.

'Guard turn out!' he shouted.

The guard of the 10th battalion of the Manchester Regiment then began to assemble.

Burge, writing later about his assault on a Manchester sentry, saw nothing strange in his inability to differentiate between Turkish and an English regional dialect.

'No wonder I couldn't understand him,' he recorded.

BALLISTIC OBITUARY

Shortly after he went to pension, Sergeant Crick of the Royal Marines Artillery followed up a newspaper advertisement and got himself a job in a circus. Circuses at the time, the early 1920's, were fiercely competitive and the proprietor of this one wanted to copy an innovation that he had heard was becoming popular in the United States.

This was the Human Cannonball. A man was fired from the muzzle of a gun into a safety-net on the far side of the arena. The proprietor reasoned that for this sort of thing you needed an expert in charge. Who better than someone of Sergeant Crick's gunnery experience?

Crick had no difficulty in recruiting a projectile. He chose a stolid and reliable former marine whose service under Crick in a

Bickleigh

succession of turrets in the Home Fleet had been exemplary.

The combination was a great success and attracted huge crowds. A miscalculation at the gun-laying end brought it to a close. The Human Cannonball soared over the top of the net, crashed into the auditorium, and broke his neck.

Asked afterwards for comment, Sergeant Crick said: 'He's a great loss. It will be very hard to find a replacement of the same calibre.'

GAME, SET AND MATCH

A 1930's batch of Young Officers, concentrated at Eastney Barracks, found itself faced with a hazard additional to the rigours of its training commitments. There was an ageing major who was a tennis zealot.

Most of the YOs played tennis and enjoyed it. They were at first pleased and flattered when the major, who on this subject at least knew what he was talking about, gave them knowledgeable help, constructive criticism and general encouragement. The major for his part assumed mistakenly that he had at last met fellow fanatics.

Things began to go wrong when he put to them collectively a proposition that for some time had been gestating slowly during most of his hours of consciousness and, in dream form, during the time when he slept.

There were four grass tennis courts in front of the officers' mess. These were entirely adequate, but they had seen long and punishing service. What the major wanted to do was to dig them up, discard the existing elderly turf, level them carefully and re-seed them. He had until now been unable to muster a volunteer labour force to do the job. Now immediately to hand, were these keen and fit young men, tennis devotees all, who would clearly like nothing better than to be given the chance to contribute to the great cause of tennis by using their spare time to refurbish the courts.

The keen and fit young men saw this scheme in a different light. They placed a high value upon their rare breaks from training which allowed them infrequent excursions to the not very alluring attractions of the pubs, cinemas and dances in Portsmouth and Southsea. They were, however, in something of a dilemma. The major had phrased his proposal as a suggestion and not as an order. It would be discourteous to decline to co-operate. He was, after all, a nice old buffer. There was a further lurking unknown quantity in their calculations. Their eventual successful passing out depended upon the cumulative marks given to them by their instructors. They were unsure about the proportion alloted to matters like initiative, keenness, energy and helpfulness. It seemed possible that if the major put forward the opinion that they were a self-centred bunch of loafers there might be unpleasant, adverse long-term consequences to their careers. The Young Officers set to work.

For an hour or so every evening they dug, carried loads of sods away in wheelbarrows, raked the soil to a fine tilth, levelled it, sweated, and thought with unexpressed resentment of the girls that they had failed to meet, the drinks that they had not had and the films that they had not seen.

The major supervised the enterprise in person. A gradual change in his attitude to his fellow workers became evident. In the beginning he had treated them as almost equals, brother labourers in the search for perfection as laid down in the specifications of the All England Lawn Tennis and Croquet Club. He slowly became more tetchy, more critical, less tolerant, more of a chain gang boss. They began to dislike him actively. They still worked dourly away.

At last the great day arrived when the seed was to be sown. The major, after consulting Wimbledon about the best strain to use, had personally bought sacks of it from a seed merchant in Gosport. He delivered it to the site in his own car. The Young Officers, who unusually because of a heavy fall of rain had been freed on the previous evening from tennis court duties and had done some shopping of their own, duly arrived and set about the seed scattering.

The major was even more pernickety and offensive than had recently become customary. He chivvied them mercilessly. He expressed dissatisfaction about the clumsiness with which they handled the heavy roller. He fussed endlessly. Then, as darkness was beginning to develop, the job was done.

The YO's straightened their backs, gathered their tools, and prepared to leave. The major made them a little speech of thanks. It was grudging, and without warmth, but at least he made it. His mind was elsewhere, ranging far ahead, beset with fantasies about a future so-far-unknown Royal Marine recruit, a natural games player from a deprived background, whose latent genius was recognised only by the major, who coached and encouraged and nurtured the lad's talent to the point where for the first time ever the Men's Singles title at Wimbledon was won by a Marine. And the whole triumphant sequence engineered here, at Eastney, by he himself, on these superb new courts that would not have existed but for his own vision and perseverance.

The major went mistily to the Mess for a drink.

*　　　*　　　*

Autumn became winter. Winter slowly changed to spring. In the early spring the batch of Young Officers who had long since left Eastney for further instruction elsewhere completed their course. They were scattered throughout the world in ship's detachments, on the China station, in the Mediterranean, in the Atlantic fleet. The major, past frictions forgotten, thought fondly of them: decent cheerful young chaps who had volunteered to do a useful job of work in their own time and who had done it splendidly, and who had left behind them a visible monument to their endeavours.

Within a few days, after the first tender green shoots began to penetrate the surface of the earth, the major discovered that a visible monument was indeed what they had left behind them. Their shopping on the evening before the courts were seeded had not been wasted. During the seeding itself there had been adroit supplementation of the grass seed. The major, with an incredulity that grew by the day, found himself contemplating the most luxuriant crop of Brussels sprouts, cabbage, curly kale, broccoli, and other assorted brassicas ever seen on a tennis court designed with loving care to meet the specifications of the All England Lawn Tennis and Croquet Club.

BILLETS DOUX

A sensible and widely enjoyed provision, economical of manpower, prevailed during the Second World War for the accommodation of Commando units in the United Kingdom. It doubtless had some highfalutin official name, but it was known as 'Civvy Billets'. The thinking behind its introduction was that every man in a Commando should be thoroughly trained to fight. If the unit were to be housed in barracks or in the innumerable hutted camps that proliferated throughout the country, a proportion of its strength would have to be diverted to the housekeeping duties of cooking, keeping the premises clean and tidy, maintenance and so on.

The alternative was to pay everyone a lodging allowance and to tell him to make his own domestic arrangements. Officers were paid thirteen shillings and fourpence a day and other ranks six shillings and eightpence. (The present day equivalents are 67p and 33p but do not of course reflect depreciated values brought about by inflation.) There were no niggling accounting requirements about how this money was spent. Anyone who could negotiate a cheaper deal with his landlady was welcome to keep the change. By the same token those willing to pay over the odds for additional luxury could do as they pleased. So long as everyone paraded when and where he was told to, correctly dressed and accoutred, no questions were asked about private lives.

Landladies were all volunteers. Their motives varied from the patriotic to the mercenary. They were of all ages and of all dispositions. They were variously kindly, motherly, rapacious, amorous, fussy, tolerant, houseproud, slovenly or anything else that landladies can be. They could also introduce some fresh, homely elements into the routine sameness of daily military living.

Unusual excuses were formulated at inspection parades.

'Dirty barrel. Take his name Sergeant Major.'

'But I *told* my landlady to use more oil with the four-by-two.'

'Still take his name Sergeant Major.'

And:

'Your cap badge is filthy.'

'Well what happened, Sir, was that my landlady was going to polish it but she used up all the Brasso cleaning the door knobs, and ...'

And:

'Those boots are disgusting.'

'Yes, I know, but I was digging up the garden for my landlady and I didn't notice how late it was and I had to double here all the way and ...'

There were some more complex by-products of the Civvy Billet system. A newly-joined subaltern reported to the adjutant of 45 Commando at Eastbourne and was told that he had been booked in provisionally to what in peace-time had been an average-sized guesthouse. He telephoned back to the adjutant within ten minutes of leaving his kit in his room. He spoke formally and in controlled tones.

'I'm in the phone box in the downstairs hall of that guesthouse you sent me to, Sir.'

'Oh yes?' said the adjutant. It seemed to him to be an irrelevant piece of information.

'The landlady is outside the box.'

This seemed to the adjutant to be, if anything, of less interest than the first sentence. He began to wonder what sort of idiot had been posted to 45. The level voice continued.

'She's stark naked and she's waving a carving knife about.'

The adjutant began to see the point of the conversation. He told the subaltern to hold on where he was. He telephoned the police station. The duty constable, once given the name and address of the guesthouse, was comforting.

'Oh, her,' he said resignedly, 'it keeps happening. It's the sight of khaki that sets her off. I'll send someone round to wrap her in a blanket.'

48

The misadventures of a troop commander, who had subsidised his lodging allowance in order to get himself installed in an elegant country hotel in Kent, were entirely of his own devising. He had, in short, severely over-dosed himself with beer before going to bed.

When he awoke, bursting to dispose of some of the beer, he found himself in total darkness. He established by touch that although he had successfully undressed he had not got as far as putting on his pyjamas. He had also forgotten where the light switch was. He felt about for it but was unable to find it. He groped his way blindly towards his *en suite* bathroom. After cracking his shins on unidentified pieces of furniture, and falling over an armchair, he became completely disorientated. He at last found a wall, ran his hands along it, reached a corner, continued to feel his way along the new wall and triumphantly clutched a door handle.

He opened the door, had a continued lack of success about light switches, and a similar tactile disappointment about the loo. He did however come across a low, hard level surface which, he considered, could only be the bath. Not a man to be deterred when an ideal solution to a problem was not immediately available he settled for a perfectly acceptable second best. He would, he decided, climb into the bath and there get rid of all that surplus beer in a relatively hygienic manner.

He placed both hands cautiously on the narrow level surface, swung his legs over and dropped into the night from the balcony outside his room. He made a fortuitously soft landing on another balcony outside another room one storey below.

His arrival made a certain amount of noise. A light went on behind the curtained window in front of him. A woman's voice said nervously: 'What was that? I heard something outside.' A man's voice, not nervous, said fiercely: 'So did I. Don't worry m'dear. I'll deal with it.'

Seconds later the curtains were dragged open violently, the door to the balcony was unlocked and an angry old man in red pyjamas stared aggressively at his nude visitor.

The visitor managed the matter with aplomb. He stepped into the room, nodded politely to a terrified-looking matron who was holding the bed clothes firmly under her chin, said with old fashioned courtesy: 'I beg your pardon. I think I must have lost my way,' and made his way out to the corridor.

At breakfast on the following morning he found a short note awaiting him from the manageress. It was propped against a flower vase on his table. It suggested that he might care to look for alternative accommodation.

The less said the better about the lodger who accidentally blew up a bathroom in Bexhill, or

50

RM Commando Initiative Test

the one who dropped a loaded Sten gun, a notoriously unstable weapon, in the downstairs hall and put a burst through his landlady's bedroom floor whilst she was sleeping, and the one who inadvertently proposed marriage to his landlady and her sister on the same evening. There are some people who never know where to stop.

But from those of us old-timers who did know that where we were stopping was a good place to be, a message: Landladies of Britain, it was all a long time ago. But we retrospectively salute you.

DOWN HILL ALL THE WAY

It took eleven days of hard fighting in September, 1943, before the beachead at Salerno, south of Naples, was secure beyond doubt. Two Commandos, No. 2 (Army) and No. 41 Royal Marine, landed at Marina on the left flank, destroyed a Coast Defence battery behind the village, cleared another village named Vietri above, and then climbed up to hold a high pass through which ran the road from Naples.

Early on in the operation Forty-One, established in positions around the La Molina defile, came under intense German mortar and machine-gun fire, protracted, an introduction to what was to become commonplace during the days ahead. Thick scrub covered the steep high slopes on either side of the pass. It was difficult to identify the observation posts from which the mortaring was being directed. Captain Chunky Stratford from 41 Commando went forward alone in an attempt to locate one of these positions. The Germans captured him.

He was taken to an observation post, high on the hillside and screened by bushes, and was held there under the personal guard of a German sergeant-major, a two-gun operator who carried his own pistol in one hand and the prisoner's in the other. After two hours the eight-man observation team withdrew, taking their prisoner with them, still under close surveillance by the sergeant-major.

The prisoner made his break from a rocky stretch of narrow path with a steep drop to one side. He suddenly bounded into the air, landed lithely some distance ahead, leapt immediately to his left, swivelled, sprang athletically to his right lower down the slope, made another brief landing, did a pirouette, and in a series of swooping, graceful mountain-goat-like leaps headed down the hill, zigzag.

He was pursued by some Wild West-type pistol shooting from the two-gun sergeant-major, and miscellaneous small arms fire from the rest of the manpower of the observation post. He was hit in the leg but kept going. The

Must be a rugged unit, that's the padre!

Germans searched cursorily for him and then gave it up. He rejoined the Commando.

He held an undisclosed advantage over his captors. In civilian life he had been a Ballet dancer.

54

RULES OF ENGAGEMENT

Within a few hours of its landing at Termoli on 2 October, 1943, P Troop of 40 Commando was faced with a problem of ethics. Termoli is an ancient fishing port on the Adriatic coast of Italy. It lies two miles north of the Biferno river, at that time the forward German defensive line. 40 Commando, No. 3 (Army) Commando and the Special Raiding Squadron were put ashore by night to seize the port, and to hold it until 78 Division of 8th Army could break through by land. The operation developed into a protracted and hard-fought battle, but the early part of it achieved total surprise. The role of 'P' Troop, commanded by Captain Gypsy Marshall, was to capture the railway station.

The distance from the beach to the station was speedily crossed. The Germans in the station were soon cleared out of it or captured. As dawn broke the Troop was comfortably established in fire positions. In front of the station was a square, about forty yards across. On the far side of the square stood a fair-sized hotel, its front covered by the weapons of Lieutenant Johnny Wisdom's platoon.

Nothing much happened until the front door of the hotel was thrown open violently, and a very large and very drunk German

55

soldier stumbled into the open. He was clutching a wine bottle in one hand, his arm fully extended horizontally. He halted jerkily, unbuttoned his trousers with his other hand, and set about relieving himself on the cobbles.

The platoon sergeant was all for shooting him. He took a relaxed deliberate aim. Wisdom stopped him.

'You can't shoot a man when he's having a pee,' said Wisdom sententiously.

'Why not?' said the platoon sergeant.

'He's helpless.'

'So what?'

'Well, you just can't do it.'

'I'm willing.'

'Well don't.'

The sergeant lowered the muzzle of his gun. The debate continued. The German soldier, swaying dangerously, grasped wine bottle still held outstretched, continued to irrigate the square. The cubic capacity of his bladder seemed to match his size.

Wisdom considered this *impasse*. He concluded that the foe would be fair game once he moved from where he was standing. The foe carried on peeing.

To speed matters along Wisdom took a rifle from the nearest marine, aimed carefully at the bottle, and squeezed the trigger. His first shot was a miss. The second shattered the bottle. The German, indifferent to these interferences, still clutching the truncated bottle by the neck, continued to pee.

A subtle shading of interest began to develop among the spectators. The philosophical argument about whether to shoot or not became secondary to speculation about how long the German could maintain his output. When the mighty flow at last diminished everyone was so mesmerised by the sheer grandeur of the performance that even the sergeant failed to get off a shot before the hero fell flat on his back through the hotel doorway.

P Troop registered the longer term tactical implications: on future operations, let the Germans know early that the merciful Wisdom was present. They would then try to ensure their personal survival by getting as drunk as they could as soon as possible.

ALL THE FOURS, FORTY-FOUR

The last, dangerous, Japanese thrust of the Burma campaign was directed at the Imphal Plain in Assam during the early months of 1944. The Japanese were beaten back after severe and prolonged fighting in and around Kohima. In the course of the battle No. 3 Commando Brigade were deployed as the mobile reserve in Assam to counter any Japanese break through. The Brigade at the time consisted of No. 1 and No. 5 Army

Commandos and 42 and 44 Royal Marine Commandos.

Two Troops of 44 Commando were sent to take up positions on Manierkhal Tea Estate. The Estate manager, Mr K. O. Smith, was a friendly and helpful Scot. He put his labour force to work to build a large *basha*, a thatched-roofed temporary construction on a wooden framework, for the use of the non-commissioned officers and marines as a canteen. Once a week a senior NCO conducted a Tombola session in the *basha*.

Tombola, or Housey-Housey, as played at that time in His Majesty's Forces, was a much noisier affair than its present-day anaemic offspring Bingo. There was no genteel, placid sitting around ticking off favourable numbers when flashed on an electronic scoreboard. In Tombola the numbers were drawn from a bag by the caller, who announced them in penetrating tones, using for the purpose a codified patter that dated from the mists of military time: All the Sixes Clicketty-Click. Legs Eleven. Number Thirteen, Unlucky for Some. Number Nine, Doctor's Orders. There was a great deal of robust audience participation: Cries of Shake 'em Up from the so-far disappointed; cheering and booing for triumphant shouters of House; and social comment when numbers came up that reflected current preoccupations and prejudices.

In the Manierkhal context the prejudices

were concerned with unit pride and intra-brigade rivalries. All the Fours, Forty Four, stimulated roars of approval and shouts of THE BEST. Number One, Number Five and Four and Two, Forty-Two, drew derisive abuse: Flannellers, Rubbish, Bullshitters.

The first evening of Tombola on the Estate attracted a large audience from the labour force. They clustered, silently bemused, around the outside of the open *basha*, unable to understand what was happening but clearly fascinated by the ritual, the noise, and the general *bonhommie*. Early on during the next week's session the marines invited them to join in. They were given a brief course of instruction in the not too demanding intricacies of play. They took to it with enthusiasm.

A few weeks later No. 3 Commando Brigade was moved on elsewhere. Forty Four thanked Mr Smith for his hospitality, and went.

Nearly fifty years later another Smith, Mr Jimmy Smith, once a sergeant in Forty Four, was packing pictures for despatch in a Gallery at St Ives in Cornwall. He noticed with interest that one was addressed to the Manierkhal Tea Estate in Assam. He was thinking about distant days when the buyer himself appeared. He was the present Estate Manager, a relatively young man for whom the Second World War was something remote, about which he had occasionally read or heard about

59

Corporal! That's the sort of thing that gets the rest of us a bad name

from his elders. There was much talk across the generations about the faraway place known to both at differing times. In the course of the discussion it came out that one at least link with the past still lingered in tea-producing circles in Assam.

The current labour force, few of whom could have been born when Jimmy Smith last set foot on the Estate, still played Tombola every Friday night. One thing about their version of the game puzzled the manager. Some numbers seemed to carry a mystic significance of unknown origin. One, Five, and Forty-Two were clearly bad. When they were called all the players booed and shouted Bollocks, Flannellers and associated Anglo-Saxon obscenities. Forty-four, on the other hand, appeared to be a number of good omen. When it came up, the players rose to their feet as one man, cheered mightily, and shouted: THE BEST. THE BEST.

STOP THAT AT ONCE

A familiar military problem that faced Commando Group in early 1944 was what to do with the Odds and Sods. These were people, Army and Royal Marine, who had recently passed out from the Depot at Achnacarry, or had recovered from wounds and were awaiting a fresh posting, or had just completed specialist courses, or were otherwise miscellaneously at a loose end. The solution chosen was to accommodate the lot in a Holding Operational Commando. It was established at Wrexham, in what had been the regimental depot of the Royal Welch Fusiliers.

The mountains of North Wales supplied a handy training area. The inmates were kept hard at it until the happy day when they moved on to a unit. The permanent staff (more accurately semi-permanent) were experienced officers and NCOs recuperating from wounds and themselves anxious to get away. They were imaginative and ingenious in dreaming up schemes that would minimise boredom and staleness. The adjutant contributed an idea with a touch of tradition.

The adjutant had been a Company Sergeant Major in the Brigade of Guards. In a mood of mixed nostalgia for his military origins, keenness to introduce something new into the proceedings, and simple vanity, he conceived a grand design. There would, he decided, be a mass ceremonial parade of the type that had once gladdened his heart on the parade ground of the Guards Depot at Caterham and, in a more refined form, on the Horse Guards' Parade in London. He fixed the first rehearsal for this event for nine a.m. on a Friday morning.

Five Troops, each man faultlessly turned

out, brasses gleaming, webbing equipment freshly blancoed, best battledress pressed to perfection, headbands of their green berets at the regulation one inch above the eyebrows, duly fell in one behind the other on their right markers. They were dressed by the right, brought their eyes to the front, and were inspected rigorously by their officers.

The parade was reported as present and correct. The two front Troops were Royal Marines, of homogeneous origin, steeped in common parade ground practices. The three rear Troops came from almost every Regiment and Corps in the British Army—infantrymen, riflemen, gunners, sappers, signallers, cavalrymen—and had interspersed at random among them members of No. 10 Inter-Allied Commando: Frenchmen, Dutchmen, Belgians, Czechs and so on, exiles from every occupied country in Europe, each indoctrinated in his own national military tradition.

The adjutant set about the fashioning of this well-meaning job lot into the sort of harmonious entity that so enchants the spectators at the Edinburgh Tattoo or the Royal Tournament.

'The Parade will Advance,' he roared vibrantly 'By the Right. Qui—i—i—ck March.'

For the first twenty yards or so all went well. The marines in front kept their alignment and strode steadily along at their regulation thirty inch paces of one hundred and twenty to the minute. Early signs of deterioration began to set in to the rear. Most of the infantry soldiers were also practitioners of one hundred and twenty paces to the minute. The Guardsmen among them, at one hundred and eighteen were slightly slower. The Riflemen, at one hundred and forty, were markedly faster.

It was unclear to anybody how the Poles and the Norwegians and the Belgians and the rest of the Inter-Allied Commando paced themselves except that it was evident that they all did it differently. Eager elements of the front rank of the third (Army) Troop soon caught up with the rear rank of the second Royal Marine Troop and began to bore into them.

At the back, in the two rearmost army Troops, there were further outbreaks of individualism. Stolid infantrymen continued to plod along at the same rate as the marines. They slowly outdistanced the Guards representatives, but were left behind by the faster movers who overtook their officers and thrust in among the more sedate marchers ahead of them; whose own sprinters were now severely harassing the steady lines of marines to their front. In less than a minute it was all beginning to look like the opening stages of a Marathon.

The adjutant had no hesitation about what

to do next. This unseemly jostling military traffic jam must be stopped at once.

'Para—a—a—a—de HALT,' he bellowed authoritatively.

When several hundred boots are crunching in unison, parade ground orders can be heard with complete clarity. When the unison is replaced by the sort of clatter made by a crowd coming out of an underground station at the height of the Rush Hour, reception is seriously diminished. Most, but not all, of the leading Royal Marine Troop, not too badly affected accoustically, heard the order clearly and crashed to a halt. So did most of the second Marine Troop, and a few of the followers-on to whom sound carried freakishly. The rest pushed forward remorselessly at their differing speeds. Resentment among the jostled grew. There were covert instances of Grievous Bodily Harm.

The adjutant tried again, this time even louder than the last.

'Par—a—a—a—de HALT,' he repeated.

Things became worse.

He was a sensible man who knew when the time had come to abandon the book.

He put his hands on his hips, threw back his head and restored the situation in a manner that would have brought heavy flushes, but some pride, to generations of his Brigade of Guards predecessors. The ghosts of many a former Royal Marine First Drill might also have nodded approvingly.

'WHOA,' roared the adjutant, 'WHOA YOU BUGGERS, WHOA.'

The Parade Whoaed.

AMATEUR STATUS

Along with the rest of the leading elements of the invasion force, 45 Commando was quarantined in a staging area for ten days before the Normandy landing. Their temporary home was on the outskirts of Southampton. In this restricted environment Marine Jock Macrae became irritable. He made an "improper remark" to a senior Non-Commissioned Officer. The NCO put him on a charge. The Commanding Officer punished Macrae by ordering that he forfeit fourteen days pay. Macrae was the MOA (Marine Officer's Attendant, the equivalent of an army batman) of Lieutenant John Day.

Four Five went ashore from Landing Craft Infantry at Sword Queen Red Beach, west of Ouistreham, on the morning of 6 June, 1944. They were shelled before and during disembarkation. During the next few days of movement, assault, counter-attack, redeployment, constant alertness and un-unremitting physical exertion they were, with unpredictable intervals of relative quiet, shelled, mortared, rocketed, machine-gunned and menaced by mines. Day's Section were in the thick of it, with Macrae a quick-thinking and reliable presence.

In a two-Troop attack on a coastal village Day was hit in the arm. Macrae bandaged him up with a field-dressing and Day continued. On the evening of the third day, after a particularly noisy German counter-attack had been repelled and another seemed likely to develop, Day and Macrae sat in their shared slit-trench with mortar bombs crashing down around them. Macrae, who for some time had been looking thoughtful, addressed himself to Day. He had to shout, to make himself heard above the pervasive racket.

'I bet,' he bellowed feelingly, 'That no other stupid bugger here's doing this for nothing.'

NORMANDY CASH CROP

The largest and most complex amphibious assault in military history was put in across the Normandy beaches on 6 June 1944. Fighting was heavy and confused. Ten days after the first landing craft had touched down, the beachhead perimeter was firmly established several miles inland.

There was still some tidying up to be done. A handful of German positions, overrun in the advance, still held out in the rear areas. One of the more formidable of these was the radar station at Douvre la Deliverand. It was a strongpoint built of heavy concrete, with living quarters, administrative offices and passageways placed well below ground. It was completely surrounded by a deep minefield sited between two continuous barbed wire entanglements.

It was a nuisance that had to be eliminated without delay. The job of reducing it was given to 41 Commando. Colonel Eric Palmer was told that he could call upon extensive support: an elaborate artillery programme, flail tanks that carried in front of them rotating chains to detonate mines, and petards that lobbed explosive charges the size of dustbins to blow in doorways and the apertures of fire positions.

Before he could prepare his assault plan in detail, Colonel Palmer needed information about the intensity of the distribution of the surrounding mines and the depth of the barbed wire thickets that abutted them. He sent out a night reconnaissance patrol led by Captain Paddy Stevens.

Stevens decided to keep it small. He took with him only a Corporal and a marine, both of whom he briefed carefully before they set out.

Stevens led them cautiously towards the front edge of the wire. Shortly before they reached it they lowered themselves gently to the ground and crawled forward on their stomachs. Stevens reached an arm silently backwards. The Corporal, well-rehearsed, passed forward the wirecutters. The marine, behind the corporal, lay alert, ready to provide support fire should anything go wrong.

Stevens patiently cut a gap wide enough to let the patrol through. There then began the tricky business of prodding for mines. Stevens inched his way forward, poking a short bayonet ahead of him into the ground at a low angle so that no downward pressure would set anything off. Some mines he neutralised. Others he skirted round. His progress became increasingly tortuous. He would need to mark his route clearly so that when the job was done he could extricate his patrol with confidence and in safety.

All members of the landing force had been issued with invasion money, banknotes of various denominations, the value of which would be honoured by the allied authorities. Stevens had a small wad of these notes in his battledress pocket. It was a windless night. At every turn in his meticulously navigated track he placed a banknote as a marker. The patrol at last reached the inner wire, Stevens in front, the corporal behind him, the marine bringing up the rear.

Stevens had found out exactly what he had come to look for. It was time to go home. The three men carefully turned themselves around in the narrow cleared channel. Stevens climbed first over the corporal's back and then over the marine's back. The corporal in turn climbed over the marine; Stevens led the way, still crawling, to the first banknote signpost. It was not there.

He had a clear picture in his mind of this part of the route. He headed for the next banknote. It too was missing. So were the third, the fourth and all the rest of them. Slowly, with deep concentration and with the help of a good memory, Stevens led his patrol safely to the outer wire and brought them back to 41 Commando's forward positions.

He reported his findings to Colonel Palmer. The 41 Commando attack, supported by an overwhelming amount of noisy and expensive paraphernalia, went in on the following day. It was entirely successful. The Germans put up a short token resistance and then sensibly surrendered.

The immediate aftermath of this triumph was soured by the premature appearance of a body of military policeman who officiously confiscated most of the large quantity of booty that had been secured. In one respect, however, Colonel Palmer kept one move ahead of the Redcaps. 41 Commando skilfully abstracted the contents of the German wine cellar.

The marine who had been the rear man of Stevens's patrol was happy, given occasionally to patting his wallet with satisfaction. It wasn't every night that when you went out on this sort of job you found money lying around at every turn.

BALKAN SHOWER

The Gulf of Kotor in Montenegro is a deep fjord of spectacular beauty backed by steeply rising limestone mountains. In the winter of 1944 advanced elements of the German 21st Mountain Corps were using the coast road from the south in an attempt to break out of the Balkans before the exits at the top of the peninsula were sealed by the advancing Russians and possibly the British from Italy.

At Risan, a small coastal town at the head of one of the inlets on the gulf, the Germans were stopped by two brigades of Marshal Tito's partisans. With the partisans was a British battery of 25-pounder guns of the Royal Artillery. Local defence of the gun positions was the task of a troop of No. 43 Royal Marine Commando.

Fighting was extensive and bloody. Partisan and German casualties were heavy. The guns were supreme. The Germans withdrew to try to make their way out by a route farther inland. The battle over, the British, to whom the Yugoslavs had offered no part in the pursuit, concentrated upon cleaning themselves up.

To the gunners this posed few problems.

71

Because of the requirements of their trade, every man travelled on wheels. There was adequate room in the transport for spare clothing, bedding and personal possessions. There was an adaptable and well-equipped pool of technicians capable of devising a variety of construction work and plumbing from unpromising materials. In the ruined upland village of Bileca they improvised a rudimentary hot shower in which they soaped themselves and soaked with gratification. When they had cleansed themselves satisfactorily, the battery commander, who had rightly given priority to his own followers, offered the hospitality of the showers to his commando escort.

The marines were in much worse hygienic condition than were the gunners. The commando scale of equipment was designed to cover the personal needs of a man on an operation lasting for a maximum of forty-eight hours. For four weeks the marines had marched over miles of mountainous country, had been drenched by violent rainstorms, and had slept wearing the only set of clothes they possessed on the earth floors of peasant cottages and livestock lean-tos. They shaved daily, washed the grime from their faces, and kept their weapons clean. Otherwise they were filthy. Some were literally lousy.

Their troop commander was Captain Bob Loudoun. When the offer of the use of the shower was put to him, he decided to give himself a rare luxury. He had raised, trained and cherished his troop. He had led it in action from the Anzio beachhead to Montenegro and had been wounded at its head in the Dalmatian Islands. He was immensely proud of his men and he took a fatherly care over their wellbeing. He would personally see to it that every one of them would wallow in the steam and soap and wash away the muck of weeks. In the meantime he would cheat.

He would start things off by taking a private shower; a prolonged, hedonistic, luxurious soaping and sluicing in limitless warm, running water whilst he thought his own undistracted thoughts, temporarily undisturbed by responsibility and concern for the followers he honoured above all men. He ordered one of his subalterns to take the troop out on a training exercise. When they returned, sweatier and dirtier than ever, they would be met by a glowing, scrubbed Loudoun, who would tell them proudly of the marvellous surprise that awaited them.

He allowed ten minutes for them to get well clear of the wrecked village. Then he rolled his towel neatly, tucked it under his arm, and walked briskly, humming to himself, to the gunners' headquarters. The gunner sentry came smartly to attention, sloped arms, and smacked the open palm of his right hand against the butt of his rifle in salute.

Home from Ascension 1908

'Good morning,' said Bob Loudoun, returning the salute.

'Morning, sir,' said the sentry.

'Where's the shower?' asked Loudoun keenly.

'They've just gone out on a training exercise,' said the sentry.

NO SODDEN AMBITION

One of the wettest places in Europe during the month of October is that part of the Montenegrin *massif* that looms above the Adriatic inlet of the Gulf of Kotor.

In October, 1944, one of the wettest people on the *massif* was Lance Corporal Harry Mingay of 43 Commando.

He was standing in a convincing imitation of an Asian monsoon. The role of the Troop that he was in was to provide local protection to a Battery of twenty-five pounder guns of the Royal Artillery who were supporting Partisan operations against the Germans. Thirty-six hours of ceaseless, driving, penetrating deluge had brought warfare temporarily to a halt. Corporal Mingay had in any case lost interest in warfare. What he was preoccupied with was thoughts of a dryness that he could see no early prospect of achieving.

He and a marine were the duty sentries on a narrow pitted track that ran about two hundred yards ahead of the gun positions. Water streamed down on them. Their green berets and the camouflage veils they wore as neck scarves were squidgy messes. Small rivulets ran down their necks. Their trousers were saturated from the knees down. Their boots squelched. Each cherished a limited damp-free zone, clearly not destined to last, underneath his gascape, a chemically treated poncho-like garment originally designed to withstand mustard gas, now universally used as a primitive macintosh. Broadly speaking, there was a shortage of happiness.

Mingay had assumed that in these circumstances he was unlikely to be bothered by traffic. He was less than delighted when a jeep splashed out of the murk and halted in front of him. From the jeep sprang a bouncy, enthusiastic person wearing what looked like a large floppy beret with a hackle attachment, an elaborate moustache, and an expression of dedicated military purposefulness. Mingay had not met him before but identified him at once by his physical appearance, a subject of *sub rosa* mimicry with a wide circulation. He was the Force Commander, a renowned fire-eating Brigadier who had distinguished himself as a battalion commander in the Irish Brigade in Tunisia, Sicily and Italy.

The dripping Mingay was at the moment in no mood to be accommodating to Brigadiers. He noted with satisfaction that this one also wore a gascape. It concealed his badges of rank and all other indications of seniority.

The Brigadier paddled aggressively towards Mingay. Foul weather or not there was only one thing foremost in this mind. He stopped, stared belligerently into Mingay's eyes, and asked a morale-boosting question.

76

'How many Germans have you killed today?' he rasped.

Mingay had been waiting for a chance like this for the past four years. He gazed gloomily at the shoulder of the Brigadier's gascape, beneath which nestled unseen a crown and three pips, and gave a considered answer.

'Haven't seen any bloody Germans today, Mate,' he said, with the air of a man always glad to share good news. He thought for a short while, and then added a postscript to make sure that there was no ambiguity about his position.

'Furthermore,' he went on, 'I hope I don't see any bloody Germans tomorrow, neither.'

SOUNDLESSNESS AND FURY

Quietly unobtrusive, matter-of-fact acts of courage and devotion to duty were what Brigadier Ronnie Tod liked. Brigadier Tod commanded No. 2 Commando Brigade in the north of Italy during the early Spring of 1945. He was on his way to the positions of No. 43 Commando in a pine wood on the Adriatic coast.

The wood, taken a few weeks previously from the Germans, was still heavily mined. Sappers had defused the mines on most of the sandy tracks and in the few open spaces that lay at intervals within the wood. That much of it was potentially lethal was indicated by thick white canvas tape that cordoned off the uncleared areas.

The Brigadier and the small group with him had reached a track junction when they heard, from ahead of them, the distant sound of German mortars being discharged. He paused briefly to apply an experienced soldier's ear to the determination of where the bombs were likely to land. There was the customary sequence of sounds: a fluttering getting louder and developing into a whistle; the whistle turning into a shriek. At some point towards the change from whistle to shriek the initiated could decide with confidence whether to carry on with what they were doing, or to flatten themselves prudently, behind cover if it was available, prostrate on the ground if it were not. This stonk, it became evident, was due to fall well short of them. The Brigadier continued to move forward.

About one hundred yards ahead of him, visible along a straight stretch of track, was a truck. It was stacked with boxes of ammunition, compo rations, drums of water and anti-personnel mines. These were being unloaded by a working party. The unloaders knew their job. A tall marine, standing in the back of the truck, methodically passed out its contents item by item to a man standing below. He in turn handed each load to the man behind him, who in turn passed it on until it was placed neatly on one of several stacks according to its nature.

This orderly routine was suddenly interrupted. The Brigadier could see clearly the men on the ground cocking their ears briefly upwards, making a correct forecast of what was to happen next and throwing themselves flat. The mortar stonk burst crashingly around them, throwing up clouds of sand and scattering severed tree branches and twigs about.

The tall man on the truck paid no attention to this distraction. He stood where he was, legs splayed, grasping a box of ammunition by its rope handles. At that distance the Brigadier was unable to hear what he was saying. There were what looked like mimed gestures of disapproval, interpreted by the Brigadier as reproaches to his less single-minded friends.

What Marine Curtis was in fact saying was: 'You lousy bastards. You've done it again. Why didn't you bloody tell me?' He said it repeatedly.

Curtis was hard of hearing. He was becoming progressively deafer. Too many things had been going bang too close to his eardrums over the past year both in Italy and in Yugoslavia. Any medical board would have repatriated him to the United Kingdom. Curtis kept clear of medical boards. He didn't want to leave the lads.

The Brigadier moved on enriched in spirit;
rightly, but for the wrong reason.

NOSE FOR DIRECTION

Coke was short and broad and strong. An
uncomplicated and helpful man, from
kindness of heart and an inability to be happy
unless physically occupied, he voluntarily did
all sorts of little things to ease the daily lives of
his companions. Coke, whistling out of tune,
put the disinfectant in the pit latrines,
unloaded more than his due share of supplies
from vehicles and took over the carrying of the
Bren towards the end of cross-country
marches.

Every military organization is better and
happier for the presence of someone like Coke.
In his case, the beneficiaries were a wartime
Royal Marines Commando troop in the
Mediterranean.

But, like many a fighting man before and
since, the hard-working, enduring,
uncomplaining, good-hearted Coke had a
weakness. Achilles, had he served in Coke's
time, would have had to be excused boots.
Napoleon's haemorrhoids are believed to have
influenced the outcome of Waterloo. The
interpretation of the orders of General Ulysses
S. Grant was a matter for careful calculation

by his staff, who had first to make a fine judgement of how sober he was when he issued them.

Coke's problem led to no strategic complications. It was local. On the not very frequent occasions when Coke had a drink or two, he would pick a fight. He chose his opponents not by the degree of offence they had given but by the simpler criterion of size. Coke's idea of an interesting evening out was to get his alcohol-bloodstream ratio properly adjusted, approach the largest man he could find, and insult him.

Not surprisingly, Coke always lost. These failures did not dispirit him.

A crisp bout with a former All Black Rugby forward from 2nd New Zealand Division, provoked into combat by Coke at the 8th Army leave centre in Bari, changed Coke's previously benign appearance for the worse. His nose, bent out of true by several degrees to its left, stayed in its new location and set there. This rearrangement brought consequential adjustments elsewhere. The right side of Coke's upper lip was pulled towards the bone and gristle it was fastened to. Coke, as simple and helpful as ever, now bore permanently an expression of sinister, leering callousness, like a mass murderer who does it for fun.

Coke was untroubled by this trans-formation. His mates were at first good-humouredly derisive and then became used to

81

it. His officers showed initial aesthetic distaste but soon realized that, properly exploited, the new-look Coke was an asset. Prisoners taken in the confusion of a commando operation on a Dalmatian Island or in an Italian battle soon became tractable when put in the care of Coke. Thoughts of escape, or reluctance to talk, withered fast at the sight of a sneering, trigger-happy sadist, cradling a Tommy gun in his arms, looking as if he was hoping for a false move that would provoke him to slaughter the lot.

Coke was equally effective with intransigent Balkan Communist political commissars. They thought twice before making ritual complaints about double-dealing capitalist allies, or the inadequacies of the Western fighting contribution compared with that of the Russian, when Coke was brought into play, strolling goonishly by in his faded green beret and his leather jerkin, a mindless, grinning psychopath drooling for blood.

Shortly after the German surrender in Italy in May 1945, No. 2 Commando Brigade returned by sea to Britain. They were to go on leave. Coke sought an interview with the unit medical officer.

Coke explained that although he himself was unconcerned by his facial expression, his girlfriend might not be. He had not seen her for two years and he wouldn't want to cause her distress. Was there any way in which the doctor could straighten out his nose and put his lip back in the right place?

The doctor was very fond of Coke. Coke had carried in wounded on his back to the regimental aid post during the Brac battle. Coke, himself shot in the shoulder, had refused to be sent back at Comacchio and had worked away, whistling, helping the medical orderlies with the other wounded. Coke had done countless unobtrusive little kindnesses for the sick and wounded in Yugoslavia and Italy.

The doctor examined Coke's bent nose. To bend it back satisfactorily would require delicate surgery and the use of sophisticated instruments not carried on the inventory of a Regimental Aid Post. The doctor told Coke that he could promise nothing but he would think it over. He would send for Coke if his thoughts led to something fruitful.

Three days later a distinguished London surgeon, responding to a request from an old pupil whom he respected, on behalf of a marine who had more than earned his pay, performed without fee an operation for which his usual run of patients would have been skinned up to their bank manager's eyeballs.

A proud and grateful Coke, swathed in dressings, brought the surgeon's notes to the unit doctor. The doctor studied the notes and told Coke that the unveiling ceremony would be in ten days' time.

The nose when finally let loose in the fresh

83

air, was a masterpiece. Coke was widely congratulated and warned jocularly that the new version was so much of an improvement on the original, let alone the interim model, that his Judy on Tyneside wouldn't recognise him.

Coke went out that night to celebrate. The largest man present in the bar of a Sussex pub was a Canadian lumberjack from a forestry company.

'No, I bloody won't,' said the doctor to Coke on the following morning, 'but at least you can tell her that it's bent round the other way now.'

ROLL OUT THE DOUBLE-BARREL

Time was, and not so very long ago, when continuous service Royal Marine officers had resonant hyphenated surnames: Tyndale-Biscoe, St Clair-Morford, Parkinson-Cumine, Cartwright-Taylor, Picton-Phillips, Wildman-Lushington. This seems to be no longer so, at least in quantity.

Ownership of this type of moniker could have its drawbacks, as was illustrated in the early summer of 1945, absent-mindedly, by Captain Shorty Roberts of 43 Commando.

Roberts and one of his subalterns were together on leave in London. After a strenuous night they went at opening time to the upstairs bar of a restaurant in Piccadilly. They were both in uniform. At that time of the day they were not feeling chatty. They sipped contemplatively at recuperative drinks and thought about their exertions ahead. They were for the moment the only customers present.

A third person arrived. He was a trim, stocky man with neatly cut greying hair and a clipped moustache. He wore a handsomely fashioned double-breasted grey pinstripe suit, highly polished shoes, a white stiff collar, and a regimental tie of vaguely Indian Army cast. He carried a bowler, a rolled umbrella, and gloves. This civilian apparatus did not, and was not intended to, leave any doubts about his profession. He might as well have been in uniform. He was in the ritualised outfit of an off-duty senior officer.

Clearly a man disinclined to squander words he hung up his bowler and umbrella, moved briskly and silently to the bar, climbed up on a bar stool and nodded to the barman. The barman said 'Good morning, Sir', mixed a carefully balanced pink gin without its being ordered, and passed it over. The new arrival nodded again, sipped at his gin, and stared ahead lost in introspection. Roberts and the subaltern looked at him appreciatively. This was the time of day when peace and quiet were welcome.

The quietness lasted until the barman, in response to a further nod, mixed a second pink gin. Then the old stager swung round on his bar stool, stared at Roberts, stared at the subaltern, and said perceptively and economically: 'Ah. Marines.' They confirmed in monosyllables that this was indeed the case. He thought things over for a while, put his ideas in order, and addressed his next remark to the subaltern.

'Do you,' he asked throatily, 'Know a chap named Arthington-Blake?'

The subaltern said no, he didn't, but Shorty Roberts might. Shorty had been in the Corps since before the war and knew all sorts of people. Roberts, who had seemed to be on the verge of falling asleep, suddenly came to life.

'Arthington-Blake?' he cried, 'Of course I know old A-B. He was in my batch.'

In so far as he allowed his controlled face to show any expression at all, the old man seemed to register a mild pleasure.

'The thing I remember most about A-B,' said Roberts expansively, 'was his colossal stamina. He was famous for it.' Roberts smiled reminiscently. The old man's face notched up a further degree of pleasure.

Recollections of good old A-B had shifted Roberts from near somnolence to something approaching volubility. 'The last time I met A-B,' he said 'was at the Holding Commando at Wrexham.'

'Training pretty hard there?' said the old man, in his most complicated sentence yet.

'Yes, I suppose it was sometimes,' said Roberts, 'But a thing I think we all admired old A-B for was an occasion when some sort of concert party, you know, dancing girls and that, came to entertain the troops. Afterwards we had the girls in for drinks in the mess. It was a large old-fashioned sort of mess. Used to be the depot of the Royal Welch Fusiliers. Hell of a party it was.'

The old man's face moved from mild pleasure to neutral. Roberts paid no attention.

'Booze was pretty hard to get at the time,' he said, 'but A-B was never put off by a handicap like that. He simply produced four bottles of Scotch. The story was that he had to sleep with a NAAFI manageress somewhere to get it. But however he did it there it was.'

Roberts chuckled. There was no stopping him now. The subaltern began to feel uneasy. The old man's face was changing to a strange mauve colour.

'Well anyway,' went on Roberts remorselessly, 'it was quite a night. A-B was generous with three of his bottles but he drank the fourth one all by himself. It didn't seem to affect him in the slightest. Of course the girls had to be out fairly early, but old A-B wasn't fussed by a thing like that.'

He chuckled lasciviously. The old man went mauver.

'The sequel to it was,' continued Roberts happily, 'that we were due to do a seven mile speed march before breakfast on the next morning. I thought that old A-B, with all that hooch inside him, might have overslept. So I went along to his room to give him a shake. And there he was, as happy as Larry, in bed with two of the girls at once.'

Roberts chuckled again. The old man's face, the subaltern noted with concern, was by now almost completely suffused.

'Then damn me,' concluded Roberts triumphantly, 'If old A-B doesn't turn out on parade as smart as paint, do the speed march as if it were a pre-breakfast stroll, and come in fresh as a daisy shouting for food. I tell you, that fellow had real stamina.'

The old man rose wordlessly to his feet. He retrieved his bowler and umbrella, and stumbled out of the door. Roberts stared after him.

'What's eating him?' he asked the subaltern.

The subaltern said that he couldn't imagine.

'Who was that fellow?' Roberts asked the barman.

'Brigadier Arthington-Blake', said the barman.

Two pubs later, when the subaltern came back from the bar carrying two pints of bitter, he found that Shorty Roberts had become pensive.

'You know that chap I was talking about

earlier on,' he said, 'The stamina man. I've just remembered. It wasn't Arthington-Blake. It was Skeffington-Hill.'

COMING DOWN TO EARTH

During the Second World War a number of Royal Marine officers served with distinction as Fleet Air Arm pilots. One of these, with a sustained record of gallantry in air operations, highly decorated, was transferred to Commandos in the first months of peace.

An early element in the training programme of the Commando course was a night exercise.

Arctic, N. Ireland, Med

This was a realistic and noisy affair with live ammunition used, tracer fired from Bren guns closely above the trainees' heads, and thunder flashes exploding in all directions.

In a very loud voice, and from a resolutely prone position, the former birdman made his views known.

'My God,' he asked, 'Is war *really* like this?'

BEST AVOIDED

Colonel Tollemache, commanding the depot at Deal in 1947, gave a welcoming address to a batch of new Young Officers on their first morning in uniform.

His closing words were: 'And finally, gentlemen, a piece of personal advise—during your service, avoid tight men and loose women.'

CUTTING THE PAINTER

The Committee's decision not to go ahead with the original choice of artist for the painting of the Commandant General's portrait was taken after an intervention by one of the junior members, the adjutant at the depot in Deal.

The portrait, to be paid for by graduated

subscriptions from all serving officers, was to be presented to the Commandant General upon his retirement. When the idea was first put to him he had endorsed it with gratitude. The gratitude had become tempered by symptoms of impatience when he was told that his presence would be welcomed at a series of sittings, each of them two hours long. Sitting still for two hours at a time had not been a distinguishing feature of his service.

The adjutant from Deal said that information had recently come to his attention that suggested that the chosen Royal Academician was not the sort of man with whom the Commandant General would care to be cooped up for any time at all, let alone two hours at a go. The information had been given in confidence and he was unable to disclose its source but he could assure the committee that it was entirely reliable. Not so long ago there had been an exchange between the painter and a potential client that had shown him, the painter, to be financially grasping, mentally obtuse, and possibly raving mad. None of these characteristics would appeal to the Commandant General.

The committee thanked the adjutant and agreed unanimously that they would have to look elsewhere for a portraitist.

The adjutant returned to Deal for tea with his informant, who was pleased to hear his news. She was his wife of six months standing.

Earlier in the week she had listened in silence whilst he told her of the planned portrait and of who was to paint it, and had surprised him by leaving the room without saying a word. She returned shortly wearing the brave and determined look of a woman about to make a disagreeable revelation.

She sat beside him and made it. Some weeks earlier she had, she said earnestly, conceived a project that she had intended to be a lovely surprise for him. She would present him with a full length portrait of herself to commemorate their first wedding anniversary. She had recently come into a modest legacy. Payment for the picture, so long as she stuck carefully to a finely calculated financial ceiling, would not be a problem.

She knew little about the art world, but a friend of hers who did had put her on to this brilliant up-and-coming young man, the youngest Member of the Royal Academy, who if not yet in the Augustus John class was clearly destined for great things. The friend added that she should not be too put out if she found the painter to be slightly dotty; dottiness was not uncommon in his profession. Also, he was surprisingly rapacious about money.

She made an appointment and called on him in his studio in Ascot. He was unremarkable in appearance, like a taciturn bank manager. Since he clearly did not relish small talk she had come straight to the point. Would he paint her portrait? Yes, he said tonelessly, for fifty guineas.

She blushed, and faltered a little, when she came to the next bit, the admission of the true nature of the lovely surprise. She had asked the artist if he would paint her in the nude. Yes, he said again in the same unemotional voice, but there would be an extra charge of five guineas for the inconvenience. She was still trying to work out what the inconvenience could be when he said: 'And there's another thing. Would you mind if I keep my socks on. I'll need somewhere to put my brushes.'

She had decided that to expose herself unclothed to a nutter like that would be asking for trouble, and had backed out of the transaction. She had meant never to mention the matter to her husband but she had thought it right to do so in view of the potential embarrassment to the Commandant General.

The adjutant admired her moral courage in speaking up as she had and told her so. He also considered some of her thinking to be slightly confused—for example, was it likely that the Commandant General would ask to be painted in the nude—but it seemed to him that there was enough evidence on offer to suggest that no chances should be taken.

He was glad that he had recommended accordingly to the Portrait Committee.

ANY OLD IRONING?

Arrangements for the reception of distinguished visitors to the cruiser HMS *Newcastle* were of the practical simplicity perfected in generations of experience by the Royal Navy. *Newcastle*, based on Malta in 1949, was making a series of friendly calls upon the ports of the French Riviera. She moored alongside the jetty at Cannes. The central element in the welcoming was a Royal Marine Guard of Honour, fallen in on the Quarter Deck. They stood motionless under the canvas awning, white helmeted, blue uniformed, brasses gleaming, boots glistening, campaign medals burnished. At their head was the recently-commissioned Second Lieutenant Mickey Denyer, conscious of the responsibilities that he was exercising publicly for the first time in his life and apprehensive about the possibility that when he saluted he might poke his sword through the awning.

The list of luminaries to be expected, and the timings of their individual arrivals, had been studied carefully. It had been accepted realistically that neither the planned order of their appearances nor the listed timings could necessarily be relied upon. Because the jetty could not be seen from the Quarter deck the ship's Commander had placed an observer on the bridge whose job was to report developments as they occurred.

His first announcements came up on schedule. 'Car approaching the gangway.'

'Car stops. French civilian gets out.'

'French civilian climbing gangway.'

The marine bugler sound the Alert. On Second Lieutenant Denyer's snapped orders the Guard of Honour crashed to attention and shouldered arms. The Frenchman, elegant in a dark suit and dark glasses, emerged onto the Quarter deck. The ship's Captain and his side party saluted. Denyer was about to give the order to present arms when the V.I.P. spoke.

'Bonjour messieurs,' he said, 'any laundry for collection?'

THE HEIGHT OF DISCRIMINATION

The Commandant General in the early 1950s was General Sir Leslie Hollis, a short trim man.

The Foreign Secretary in the early 1950s was Mr Ernest Bevin, a short fat man.

Mr Bevin, regarded by many experienced Foreign Office officials as the best Foreign Secretary they had dealt with in their working lifetimes, had begun his career as a Trade Union organiser of notable belligerence and had sensibly seen no reason to try to adapt his approach and personality when he moved into

Have you given this marriage much thought, Wilkins?

the highest levels of national and international politics. He did not beat about bushes. He trampled them into the ground with an earthy realism and pithy commentaries expressed in an accent that made no concessions to the inclusion of inconvenient aitches.

In 1950 Mr Bevin, in Egypt upon official business, took passage in HMS *Kenya* from Suez to Ceylon to attend the Colombo Plan Conference. When *Kenya* was well into the Indian Ocean the wardroom entertained Mr Bevin to dinner on the quarterdeck. Lieutenant Guy Woods, of the Royal Marine detachment, was seated next to the Foreign Secretary.

It early became evident that for many a long year Mr Bevin had nourished a deep grievance about the Corps. He looked carefully at the insignia on Woods's mess jacket and spoke his mind.

'Would you believe it?' he said, 'I tried to join the Royal Marines, but they turned me down. Said I was too short. And when I met your 'ead man 'Ollis I couldn't 'elp saying to 'im—'Ow come a little runt like you could get in when they turned me down for being too short?'

MONKEY WRENCH

Rosie, named after the colour of her bottom, was an ill-favoured, short-tempered, jealous, inquisitive, interfering, neurotic monkey who lived in a tree in the garden of the Bachelors' Mess in Tapah. A long, light steel chain, linking her to a forked branch, was fastened to a belt around her waist. She passed much of her time squatting contemplatively in the tree, doing disgusting things to herself. There were occasional sudden outbreaks of frantic, chain-rattling, activity, during which she swung around the branches hysterically and dived with menaces at any human sufficiently rash or sufficiently ill-informed to approach the tree too closely. Since the tree abutted the parking space in front of the bungalow she found plenty of attractive targets and achieved, from her point of view, many satisfying successes.

Her only friend was her owner and patron, the Officer in Charge of the Police District, a former Parachute Regiment officer. From time to time this otherwise worldly cynic would unchain Rosie, bring her into the bungalow, clasp her to his bosom, stroke and fondle her, and talk drivelling nonsense to her in the manner of a young mother with her first baby. These recurrent outbreaks of gooey sentimentality irritated one of the other

98

occupants of the Mess, the Assistant District Officer, a one-time marine. He found it nauseating and said so, frequently.

* * *

After dinner on a night in 1951 the OCPD and the ADO sat in bamboo armchairs, sipping their coffee and wondering what to argue about next. Outside there was a tropical storm of great intensity, unusual but not unknown in after-dark Malaya. Most Malayan storms were afternoon affairs. This one generated spectacular flashes of lightning, crackling thunder, and a downpouring of tropical rain that drummed noisily on the roof and splashed up nearly as noisily on the gravel driveway and the shrubs in the garden. The ADO opened a book. The OCPD, in defiance of the clamorous sounds of nature, started up Doris Day on the record player. The telephone rang.

Ten minutes later a saturated Chinese Special Branch officer arrived with an informer. The informer was an unprepossessing young Chinese, dressed in a sodden shirt and slacks. He was in it for the reward money. The OCPD, who took his professional duties seriously and who looked upon avaricious Judases as a rare bonus to be cherished, gave the man a glass of orange juice, treated him with punctilious courtesy, fetched a map, and together with the Special Branch inspector began a detailed cross-examination. The ADO was uninvolved in detailed police business. He considered the informer to be as repulsive as the monkey Rosie, now lodged damply in her tree. He distanced himself from the discussion by taking his book to a chair at the far end of the room.

After several minutes of interogation the OCPD moved to the telephone and put a call through to the local military unit, No. 45 Royal Marine Commando. Security ruled that he spoke elliptically, but he made it clear that he had some reliable information that required immediate action. He hung up the telephone and returned to the informer.

Minutes later there was the sound of a jeep skidding to a halt in the pounding rain. Major Jack Richards, the second-in-command of 45 Commando, and the Commando Intelligence Officer came wetly into the bungalow. They had, they said, broken the course record from Temoh Hill camp. What was this urgent information?

The informer, explained the OCPD, was a member of the *Min Yuen*, the Communist organisation that backed up the Communist terrorists by supplying them with food, medicines and information. He had that afternoon attended a *Min Yuen* meeting in a Resettlement Village at the foot of the Cameron Highlands road. A terrorist food-lift party was due to come to the village that same night. The informer, who had himself taken part in the planning, knew the precise point at which the terrorists would breach the perimeter wire fence. The OCPD had marked this spot on a simple sketch map that he had devised, and the informer had confirmed its accuracy. The only gap in the informer's knowledge was to do with timing. He knew only that the food collectors would come at some time during the night. Speed was essential if a Commando ambush party were to hit the target.

Jack Richards and the Intelligence Officer agreed without further comment. They strode out to the still-unabated downpour, climbed into their jeep, and drove away.

During the night there were a number of telephone calls, not unusual to an operational police officer in one of the roughest Districts in Malaya during the worst year of the Emergency. At breakfast on the following morning the OCPD and the ADO had a row. One of the telephone calls, said the OCPD bitterly, had come from 45 Commando. They had arrived too late. The birds, and the food that they had lifted, had flown. This, said the OCPD, was a bloody disgrace. Four-Five were an incompetent, idle, slow-moving shower. They had had ample warning to put an ambush party in place. If they'd been any good they'd have got the lot.

The ADO was not prepared to accept

unchallenged this slur on his old unit. He said the OCPD was talking cock. The ADO had only half listened to the conversation of the previous evening, but one point that he had picked up was that the informer was uncertain of the time when the bandit food-lift party was due to put in an appearance. Instead of making a lot of stupid accusations based on inadequate evidence, the OCPD could better use his time by finding out what had actually happened. Breakfast ended in sulphurous silence.

Later in the morning Major Jack Richards set the record straight with one succinct sentence: 'We were late,' he said to the OCPD, 'because your bloody monkey ate our windscreen wipers.'

STABLE BACKGROUND PREFERRED

As is customary on these occasions, all events on the programme of the 1956 Edinburgh Tattoo were rehearsed rigorously and timed to the second. For obvious reasons of economy one component of the *finale* on the last night, an elaborate and expensive firework display, was not given a pre-show run through. When the manoevres that the fireworks would accompany were being practised, the parade's co-ordinator checked his clipboard and his stop watch and announced that fireworks would start here or end there as the case may be.

As the climax to the last night approached, the applause from the spectators became progressively more enthusiastic. Under floodlights, in the shadow of Edinburgh Castle, the Royal Marines King's Squad put on a faultless display of drill, the massed pipes of the Highland Regiments and the Royal Marines Band played Scotland The Brave, participants in earlier events from all services joined the parade smartly, and the parade commander, the Royal Marines adjutant, mounted on a beautifully turned out horse, called the parade to attention.

The pyrotechnics were next. The adjutant had been unsure of the likely reaction of the horse to the fireworks, and he had planned accordingly. A horse handler discreetly moved into position and took a firm grip on the reins close under the bit. The parade stood still, glittering magnificently in the floodlights. The spectators fell silent. Timed to the second, rockets soared into the air from the castle battlements and lit the night sky with shining clusters of brilliance. There were protracted thunderous bangs closer to the earth. Falling rain tumbled spectacularly down the castle walls. The adjutant's horse, controlled by him, gentled by the handler, showed mild signs of agitation but remained motionless.

There was a pause before the national

A Horse Marine

I think we would find it more convenient to review the troops on *foot*

anthem. The horse handler removed himself from the scene as unobtrusively as he had arrived. This was a mistake. On the first musical bar, which was accompanied by the first of the final illuminations, the horse decided that it had enough. It headed for the High Street carrying the adjutant with it. There was some subsequent dispute about when the horse, with its accompanying adjutant, reached its stable in Holyrood Palace. The generally accepted version was that their joint arrival coincided with the playing of the last of the national anthem.

RED BERET BOTTOM LINE

In matters of publicity the adjutant of No. 43 Commando was a resourceful man. He did not let his enthusiasm carry him quite so far as did some of his American opposite numbers. But he knew a good thing when he saw one.

An impending good thing in 1967 was the imminent arrival in the harbour at Plymouth of Francis Chichester in Gypsy Moth. Chichester had just completed a single-handed circumnavigation of the globe, an achievement that had rightly attracted massive international press and television attention.

The welcome awaiting him, both planned and spontaneous, was elaborate. Sailing craft of all sizes congregated in Plymouth Sound, with a view to meeting Chichester on the last leg of his journey and escorting him triumphantly home. Television crews from the world over were there to record the event. To impose some sort of maritime traffic control on a potentially over-crowded situation 43 Commando were asked to man two inflatables which would guide the traveller through the throng.

The adjutant was pleased with his preparations for the exploitation of this public relations opportunity. He put painters to work. Television viewers, he later told an appreciative audience of his fellow officers in the mess, could not fail to identify who among the celebrating welcomers were doing a practical and necessary job of work. ROYAL MARINES had been painted in clear large letters on both sides of the inflatables and on their jumping boards. Any camera, from any angle, at eye level or from the air, would get the message which would be absorbed by millions of viewers.

Only one of the adjutant's listeners was unimpressed. He was a Parachute Regiment Officer seconded to the Commando and he considered it high time to puncture all this complacency.

'What happens,' he asked sardonically, 'when you capsize?'

'I've had PARACHUTE REGIMENT

painted on the bottoms,' said the adjutant.

DOING IT BY THE BOOK

A British Colonial ritual of long standing was the signing of the Governor's book. The book, a large volume, not unlike that used by guests checking into hotels, was housed in an outer office of the Residency. Visitors of standing, who wished to pay their respects to the Governor, and who did not wish to bother him personally any more than he wished to be bothered by them, called to fill in their names, addresses, and the duration of their stay in the territory.

Respects aside, it was a practical arrangement. The book was inspected daily by the Governor's Private Secretary, who then used its contents to prepare lists of people whom he judged that the Governor would like to meet personally, and of these who should be included in guest lists for dinners, luncheons, or receptions. Service officers were instructed that as a matter of courtesy they should regard themselves as automatic book-signers.

In 1963, 42 Commando were engaged in operations in Sarawak. Overall operational control was exercised by a committee presided over by the Governor. It was impressed upon all ranks, particularly to those reinforcements new to the Far East, that a high standard of security was essential if operations were not to be prejudiced. The Asian gossip grapevine was impressively effective.

The Governor's Private Secretary, doing his daily check of the Book in the residency in Kuching, read entries by two officers from 42 Commando.

Under the heading Date of Departure the first had written: You should know! The second had confined himself to: Careless talk costs lives.

A ROSE BY ANY OTHER NAME IS STILL A LEEK

When, after more than thirty years of distinguished service, Colonel Dai Morgan retired from the Corps he was still a mentally and physically active man of wide experience with many years of active work still in him.

One of the several jobs for which he applied was that of the newly created post of administrative secretary to the Rugby Union. The Rugby Union, the arbiters, legislators and organisers of English Rugby, had its headquarters at Twickenham. The aim of the new job was to take some of the weight of the workload from the shoulders of the full-time Secretary. The conditions were attractive—

good salary, subsidised house and motor car, travel abroad with touring English teams, free seats available for every international match played at Twickenham. The new incumbent would also have available to him a small reserve supply of international tickets that he could allocate personally to deserving people who had helped further the interests of the game in England.

Colonel Morgan's application was successful. He applied himself energetically and with enjoyment to his new duties. There was however one minor matter that caused him some concern. It was the era during which Welsh Rugby was dominant in the international scene, the time of the great names of Gareth Edwards, Phil Bennet, J. P. R. Williams, Mervyn Davies and the incomparable rest of them. The English side, along with those of the other non-Welsh contenders for the Five Nations Championship, were annual victims of Welsh skill, speed, guile and general superiority. Would it not be felt in some English quarters for it to be well, er, provocative for a senior official of the English Rugby Union to have a name, in these Welsh triumphalist times, like Dai Morgan?

Colonel Morgan let it be known discreetly to his old marine friends that he would prefer it if in future they would cease to address him as Dai and instead would call him Denis Morgan.

Up here, you b . . . . . nit!

His friends did indeed alter the nomenclature, but not quite in the way he wished. They now called him Dai The Ticket.

WINGS AND NOGGS

A Royal Air Force pilot with the melancholy record of having spent more time than almost anyone else in German Prisoner-of-War camps between 1939 and 1945 was Wing Commander H. M. A. Day. He was shot down over Germany on Friday, 13 October, 1939 whilst leading a reconnaissance flight of Blenheim aircraft.

He was forty-one years of age at the time of

110

his capture. His service seniority made him an automatic choice as Senior British Officer in the several camps in which he was incarcerated. His undeviating policy in these, which he enforced by sheer strength of personality among boisterous aircrew-captives most of whom were half his age and over none of whom he held any practical disciplinary sanctions, was to be as cooperative as could be with the German camp staff, whilst at the same time encouraging and supporting every feasible escape attempt. He himself got through the wire on a number of occasions, after each of which he was recaptured.

In 1944 he was the moving spirit and a participant in the mass breakout from the camp at Sagan, which led notoriously to the murder by the Gestapo of fifty retaken RAF escapers. Wings Day, taken yet again, was sent to Sachsenhausen concentration camp. He escaped from there too, with a group of similarly bloody-minded British officers, and made his way to the American lines in Italy as the war was drawing to its close.

The Service career of Wings Day (not yet known as Wings) began when he was commissioned as a Probationary Second Lieutenant in the Royal Marine Light Infantry in 1916. His early time was at sea. He was in the battleship *Britannia* when she was torpedoed and he was awarded the Albert Medal, subsequently replaced by the George Cross, for struggling through heavy smoke and cordite fumes to rescue two men trapped below decks. ('One was the wardroom steward. I wanted the bar keys.')

He took to flying in 1924, initially on secondment to the Fleet Air Arm, later on permanent transfer to the Royal Air Force. He was dedicated to his new Service. But he never forgot his Royal Marine origins, and the discipline and leadership by example that helped him immeasurably to inspire the morale and cohesion of the thousands of prisoners for whom he was responsible.

* * *

In the early 1970s an ageing Wings Day, after making an appointment by telephone, presented himself in the office of the Major General, Royal Marines, at Eastney Barracks at Portsmouth. Carried casually in one of Day's hands was a small earthenware jar. He chatted reminiscently and inconsequentially for a short while and then put the jar on the desk in front of him.

'Noggs Fiennes,' he said abruptly.

General Bob Loudoun did not know what to make of this. He wasn't even sure what language was being spoken.

Wings Day elaborated. He had, he said, just returned from the United States. He had brought with him the ashes of his old Royal

112

Marine friend, Major "Noggs" Fiennes. The ashes were in the jar. Old Noggs had asked that they be scattered in the English Channel.

Wings had made two abortive attempts to carry out this last wish. The first had been at the end of Eastbourne pier. Wings had carried the jar the length of the pier, had removed the lid, tested the wind and then hesitated. 'Couldn't just dump old Noggs in like that.' Something more appropriate, with suitable service connotations, seemed to be required. Wings took the jar back along the pier again.

Some days later, still carrying the jar about with him, Wings came up with a better solution. He explained his predicament to a nephew of his, a pilot in the Army Air Corps. The nephew listened sympathetically. He offered to take his uncle up in an aircraft, fly him over the Channel and circle while Wings put the ashes over the side. Wings accepted the offer gratefully, but here again last minute second thoughts intruded. The nephew was his nephew and was kind and considerate, but when all was said and done he was still a Pongo. 'Anyhow, Noggs didn't like flying.'

Would General Bob, asked Wings shyly, giving the jar a prod with his forefinger, consider arranging a proper sort of Corps send off for old Noggs?

General Bob had no reservations about doing so. With ceremony, and to the accompaniment of the Last Post played by a

113

It says: 'Mind you don't catch cold—*signed Royal Marines*

Royal Marine bugler, the ashes of old Noggs were scattered in the English Channel from the deck of the Admiral's Barge of the Naval Commander-in-Chief, Portsmouth.

DROP IN THE OCEAN

The official designation of merchant ships requisitioned in time of war or national emergency is Ships Taken Up From Trade, abbreviated to the acronym STUFT. The largest ship to be STUFT for the Falkland Islands expedition in 1982 was the P&O liner S.S. *Canberra*. She carried 42 Commando, most of 40 Commando, a company of 45 Commando and the third battalion of the Parachute Regiment. Her promenade deck was adapted to a helicopter pad, and was in constant use for physical training by the troops. There was much hard marching ahead of them. It was essential that they kept as fit as was possible.

The troop accommodation was several decks below. In its more elegant cruising days, *Canberra's* paying passengers completed their relaxations on the promenade deck and then made their way decorously to cabins, bars or restaurants by a set of lifts of limited capacity. Maximum numbers acceptable were listed on notices displayed within the lifts.

Unimpressed by this civilian fussiness, about twenty marines, PT over, crowded into one of the after lifts and lavishly exceeded the recommended tolerable poundage. The lift hurtled to the bottom of the lift shaft at a speed never before recorded and was wrecked. No marines suffered physical damage, but they were emotionally affronted when all lifts were at once put out of bounds to all embarked troops.

3 Para put forward a professional judgement upon this episode: 'If the marines want to try Free Fall jumping they might at least remember their bloody parachutes.'

RESTRAINT ON TRADE

Naval Party 8901, the designation of the Royal Marines detachment, forty-one strong, who constituted the entire Defence Force of the Falkland Islands and which customarily faced no realistic enemy threat from anyone, found itself at war on 2 April 1982. After several weeks of sabre rattling, counter propaganda and high level international bickering, the Argentines made an amphibious landing at Port Stanley at six o'clock in the morning.

The marines manned their pre-selected defensive positions in and around Government House, the official residence of Sir Rex Hunt, the Governor. They were soon engaged in a heavy fire fight with Argentine troops who outnumbered them and outgunned them several times over.

Bullets zipped through and over the house, and ricocheted off the road in front of it. In the midst of all this, Marine Turner, a member of the team commanded by Regimental Quartermaster Sergeant Aspinal, saw a man approaching on foot. He was carrying a white flag and making his way towards Port Stanley.

Turner at once became a principal in two short conversations, one after the other.

Turner to Aspinal: 'RQ, there's a bleeding civvy walking down the road.'

Aspinal to Turner: 'Tell him to go away.'

Turner to civilian: 'Oy, you. Bugger off. Can't you see what's going on?'

Civilian to Turner: 'It's all right for you lot. Some of us have got to go to work.'

IT'S BEEN AN ANXIOUS TIME

Argentine troops had been in occupation of the Falkland Islands for forty-nine days when, in the early hours of May 21 1982, the first landing craft from the British Amphibious Task Group touched down near San Carlos Settlement in the north west of East Falkland. 40 Commando landed on Blue Beach One.

Each man, face and hands blackened with camouflage cream, was heavily loaded with weapons, ammunition and equipment. They moved rapidly inland to the north and east to secure their first objectives, the reverse slopes of a broken line of high hills that ran parallel to the deep inlet of San Carlos Water. There they dug in, after clearing the intervening ground and hoisting the Union Flag over the Settlement.

Intelligence about Argentine strengths and locations was scanty. During the night there had been considerable uproar to 40 Commando's left, when the Special Boat Squadron drove back a half company strong Argentine Force known as the Fanning Hill Mob and the Third Battalion of the Parachute Regiment dealt similarly with the other half of the Argentine company which had been based near Green Beach One. 40 Commando's immediate area was thought to be reasonably enemy-free; but no chances could be taken. From first light onwards the observation posts along the crests of the hills, and patrols pushed out ahead, looked with suspicion at any sign of human movement and took precautionary measures to deal with it should it prove to be hostile.

One human, his movements covered comprehensively by the weapons of business-like marines, was dressed in civilian clothes. He seemed to be an islander but conceivably could

118

be some sort of Argentine spy. Whatever he was, he clearly had something on his mind. Unintimidated by the gun muzzles, the green berets and the blackened faces, he strode forward purposefully until he was within easy chatting range. Once there he wasted no time on greetings, introductions or other conventional civilities. What he wanted was information.

'Have Leeds United been relegated?' he asked tensely.

BOMBS AWAY SOMEWHERE OR OTHER

3 Commando Brigade Royal Marines, who early developed a respectful dislike for the

Falklands 1982
Dashed hard luck on the sailors, eh chaps?

efficiency and courage of the aircrew of the Argentine Air Force, were greatly cheered when Vulcan aircraft of the RAF put in a bombing strike on the Argentine-held airfield at Port Stanley. Their pleasure was modified when reconnaissance photographs showed that out of forty-two bombs dropped, forty-one had missed the runway.

Some days later a letter from home arrived for a marine. It described in enthusiastic detail a visit to the Air Day at RAF Halton. The most thrilling part of these festivities, recorded the sender, had been a re-enactment by two Vulcans of the bombing of the Stanley airfield.

The marine's response to this part of the letter was brief: 'How many spectators were killed?'

WOMEN AND DRINK

After the inevitable surrender to the Argentines of the small Royal Marines detachment defending Government House in Port Stanley, it was agreed that the prisoners would be repatriated to Britain. They were taken to Montevideo and put up in the Hotel Castello. It was a large, old and rather grand establishment. Its bar stocks were ample, but the marines had no money. All they had in the world was the clothing that they had been wearing at the time of capture.

The Company Sergeant Major entered into negotiations with the hotel manager. The bar would accept chits over signatures with a clearly printed name below. The final total bar bill would be underwritten by the British Government.

When the time came to leave the bill was submitted to the officer commanding the detachment. He found that the heaviest drinkers for whom he was responsible were Mrs Margaret Thatcher and Queen Victoria.

THE BURDEN OF HISTORY

The last tour of a hot day was by a party of Americans, avid for knowledge. Marine Simkin, their guide, thinking wistfully of the refreshments that he would head for as soon as this lot was over, led his charges competently around Nelson's flagship, HMS Victory, in Portsmouth dockyard.

He had mastered his brief well. They were impressed by his grasp of detail, the depth of his insight into what naval life was like during the Napoleonic wars, his interpretation of the events of that distant day off Cape Trafalgar, and the courteous readiness with which he replied to questions.

The day was getting hotter. Simkin's first

beer was getting closer. He led them finally to the Orlop deck, deep in the bowels of the ship. Here, for the first time, he drifted away from the script.

'This,' he said, 'is the Orlop, to which the famous marine sergeant Secker carried Lord Nelson after he had been struck down by a French musket ball on the upper deck. It was a great struggle for the sergeant and I can tell you, ladies and gentlemen, that we, the Royal Marines, have had the bloody Navy on our backs ever since.'

COOKERY CLASS

The Commandant General, who valued precision, put random snap questions in the course of his inspection of Headquarters Company of 42 Commando.

'What do you do?' he asked a marine.

'Chef, Sir.'

'Have you passed your City and Guilds examination?'

'No Sir.'

'Then you're not a Chef. You're a Cook.'

Further along the line he asked another marine what he did.

'Cook, Sir.'

'How long have you been a cook?'

'About forty seconds, Sir.'

Perhaps we're a major item of kit and due for exchange as part of this kit upkeep allowance scheme!

THERE'S AN EAR IN THE WALL

It was bound to happen sooner or later and it was Laura, fastidious, shy, easily-embarrassed Laura, who uncharacteristically precipitated the decision.

Would Charles, she said, kindly bend his cultivated brain and his organisational talents to working out where they could do It in suitable anonymity and comfort? Comfort was important. She was not talking of monkeying about in the rear seats of motor cars.

Charles was a quick mover who had recently completed the two-year officer qualification course. He was by habit and training a noter of present irrelevancies that might in the unforseeable future be put to good use. During the following week he examined his memory and came up with a winner.

On a reconnaissance exercise on Dartmoor he had once, from behind cover, looked with interest through binoculars at an isolated hotel tucked away in a charming little valley. One of its features that had stuck in his mind was the presence of a number of small children. There were swings and slides and see-saws, riotously patronised in a well-cherished garden. In his experience the English did not take kindly to children in hotels. Curious, he had later made enquiries. The hotel, exceptionally, catered for

124

families and provided everything that would ease the burden of parenthood for its customers.

He thought it over. It became clear to him that the remoteness of the hotel and its preoccupation with children combined the advantages that he was looking for. Neither he nor Laura was known there. The fathers and mothers, however much their tasks were moderated by the hotel's proprietors, would have their minds primarily upon their children. They would be unlikely to be diverted into nosiness. Over a cup of coffee he put this appreciation of the situation to Laura. She said that she had never admired him more.

Mr and Mrs John Smith booked themselves in for the weekend. A girlfriend of Laura's was enlisted to provide traditional cover from her father and mother to say, if telephoned, that Laura was staying with her. They enjoyed the drive across one of the last expanses of the south of England unsullied by mankind. They, Laura in particular, were slightly nervous at the reception desk but they were greeted pleasantly, signed in, and were handed a key. Room No. 6, first floor up the stairs, third door on the right. Times of meals listed on a card on the bedside table. Enjoy your stay.

They wasted no time over checking the times of meals. They set about enjoying their stay. The early stages of doing It developed very well, and with a growingly noisy volume of

125

mutual appreciation expressed not only in words. A setback came when matters were well under way.

They slowly became aware of a loud, persistent, rhythmic hammering sound. Laura was so naive that she assumed it to be an integral part of the proceedings. Charles at last identified it. Somebody was beating on the door, hard. He cursed, got out of bed, wrapped himself in a bath towel and went to the door. It was the receptionist.

'Would you mind,' she asked frostily, 'switching off the Baby Intercom? It's the red switch on the wall just above the telephone. You've been broadcasting in the bar, the residents' lounge and the reception area for the past ten minutes.'

RESPONSIBLE PARENTHOOD

Until events in the Soviet Union in the late 1980's altered the nature of the threat to Western interests, one of the units of No. 3 Commando Brigade spent much of its time in Norway, the northern flank of the defensive arrangements of the North Atlantic Treaty Organisation. There the marines did their Arctic and Mountain Warfare training, exercised in the snow and ice, and developed an affection for their Norwegian allies. One of the manifestations of this goodwill came one Sunday when the long winter was coming to an end and the first signs of spring were in the air. A party of marines decided to attend Divine Service in a small, rural Norwegian church.

The worshippers faced one obvious difficulty. Their knowledge of the language, where it existed at all, was rudimentary. Although they would be united in sentiment with their Norwegian hosts their understanding of the detailed proceedings of the morning would be, to put it at its lowest, sketchy. The associated problem of when to stand up, kneel down, or sit was fairly easy to deal with. They would follow the well-established procedure put to use by people who attend the wedding and funeral services of friends who belong to denominations other than their own: Keep an eye on the initiated and do as they do. To minimise the chance of error the marines congregated in a solid block at the rear of the church.

For most of the Service they did not put a foot wrong. They stood, knelt and sat with carefully observed timeliness. When, as they understood it, the ceremony was approaching its close and they, in conformity with the moves of the rest of the congregation, were sitting down, the pastor made a short address.

A man in a pew towards the front stood up. About thirty marines stood up too. The remainder of the people in the church, still

Once moor before supper

seated, turned around and stared, looking mildly astonished. Young girls giggled discreetly. Young men sniggered. The marines stood their ground stolidly. When the solitary man at the front sat down so did the marines.

Outside the church, the service over, they asked one of the many English-speaking Norwegians about the cause of this little contretemps.

'What the pastor said,' explained their friend, 'was: Will the father of the child who is to be christened on Monday please stand up.'

JUST DESERTS

Apologised to for being described in the Junior Minister's after-dinner speech as of the Royal American Marines, the visiting United States Marine Corps General was urbanity itself.

'Perfectly natural slip of the tongue,' he said easily, 'And anyhow it's more or less historically accurate. Our Marines were originally formed from deserters from your Marines.'

Ranks not allowed!! beyond this point when firing

DEAD RINGER

In 1989, when the intransigency of President Saddam Hussein of Iraq over Kuwait made war inevitable, Captain Saberton-Skinner, with a small detachment of marines, was sent on special duties to the Gulf. His task, still on the secret list, was behind the Iraqi lines. As was his custom he carried it out with distinction. It lasted for several weeks. When it was over, and his detachment was withdrawn, he at last found himself in a position to be able to telephone his wife.

There was some delay, which he found irritating. He was arrogant and rich and intolerant of inefficiency. He finally got through. The line crackled badly.

'Butler,' said a voice.

'I want to speak to my wife' said Saberton-Skinner, peremptorily.

'I'm afraid she's not available, Sir.'

'Why not?'

'She's upstairs in bed with your best friend.'

'Oh,' said Saberton-Skinner. He thought briefly. Then:

'Go to my study,' he said, 'and take out my shotgun. Load both barrels. Then go upstairs and shoot the two of them. When you've done it come back and report to me. I'll keep the line open.'

'Sir!'

Saberton-Skinner listened carefully. He could hear the swishing sound of movement, the cautious opening and shutting of the study door, its reopening, and muffled footsteps on the stairs. There were two loud bangs, one immediately after the other. There was further swishing, a short delay, and resumed conversation on the line.

'All done Sir.'

'Good. What did you do with the gun?'

'I threw it in the swimming pool.'

'Swimming pool? What swimming pool? Is that 027844...?'

Withdrawal from Aden—1967
'All right lads, the usual routine—half a dozen bars of the old "Retreat", haul down the flag, and beat it back to the beach. We'll skip the "slow march" bit today 'cos we're a bit pressed for time...!

IT'S FOOTWORK THAT TELLS

After he became Commandant General in 1949 General Sir Leslie Hollis reflected upon the great volume of well-meant advice that had been given to him by senior officers when he was a young subaltern.

Only one of these maxims remained firmly in his memory: Never fornicate in suede shoes. It makes the toecaps shiny.